McMaster University

Pauline John

E. Pauline Johnson

Betty Keller

Betty Keller lives in Sechelt, British Columbia. She has worked as a teacher, editor, writer, and literary arts producer, and she is a mentor to other writers. But Betty Keller is best known as the founder and producer of the Sunshine Coast Festival of the Written Arts (Sechelt Writers Festival). She held this position from 1983-1994.

Her publication record is impressive, both as writer and more recently as ghost writer or editor. Her earlier book, *Pauline: A Biography of Pauline Johnson*, won the Canadian Biography medal for 1982. Other books by Betty Keller include *Black Wolf: The Life of Ernest Thompson Seton*; *On the Shady Side: Vancouver 1886-1914*; *Bright Seas and Pioneer Spirits: The Sunshine Coast*; *Sea Silver: Inside British Columbia's Salmon Farming Industry*; and *Forests, Power and Policy: The Legacy of Ray Williston*.

THE QUEST LIBRARY
is edited by
Rhonda Bailey

Editorial correspondence:
Rhonda Bailey, Editorial Director
XYZ Publishing
P.O. Box 250
Lantzville BC
V0R 2H0
E-mail: xyzed@bc.sympatico.ca

In the same collection

Lynne Bowen, *Robert Dunsmuir: Laird of the Mines*.
Dave Margoshes, *Tommy Douglas: Building the New Society*.
John Wilson, *Norman Bethune: A Life of Passionate Conviction*.
Rachel Wyatt, *Agnes Macphail: Champion of the Underdog*.

Pauline Johnson

Canadian Cataloguing in Publication Data

Keller, Betty

Pauline Johnson : first aboriginal voice of Canada

(The Quest Library ; 3)
Includes bibliographical references and index.

ISBN 0-9683601-2-2

1. Johnson, E. Pauline (Emily Pauline), 1861-1913. 2. Poets, Canadian (English) – 19th century – Biography. 3. Mohawk Indians – Canada – Biography. I. Title. II. Series.

PS8469.O289Z732 1999 C811'.4 C99-941368-6
PS9469.O289Z732 1999
PR9199.2.J64Z732 1999

Legal Deposit: Fourth quarter 1999
National Library of Canada
Bibliothèque nationale du Québec

XYZ Publishing acknowledges the support of The Quest Library project by the Canadian Studies Program and the Book Publishing Industry Development Program (BPIDP) of the Department of Canadian Heritage. The opinions expressed do not necessarily reflect the views of the Government of Canada.

The publishers further acknowledge the financial support our publishing program receives from The Canada Council for the Arts, the ministère de la Culture et des Communications du Québec, and the Société de développement des entreprises culturelles.

Chronology: Lynne Bowen
Layout: Édiscript enr.
Cover design: Zirval Design
Cover illustration: Francine Auger

Printed and bound in Canada

XYZ Publishing
1781 Saint Hubert Street
Montreal, Quebec H2L 3Z1
Tel: (514) 525-2170
Fax: (514) 525-7537
E-mail: xyzed@mlink.net

Distributed by: General Distribution Services
325 Humber College Boulevard
Toronto, Ontario M9W 7C3
Tel: (416) 213-1919
Fax: (416) 213-1917
E-mail: customer.service@emailgw.genpub.com

Pauline JOHNSON

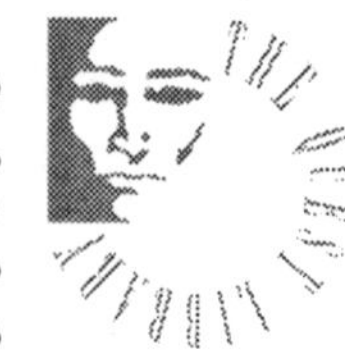

FIRST ABORIGINAL VOICE OF CANADA

Contents

1 The Star of the Show 1
2 The Aboriginal Voice 13
3 The Toast of London 29
4 On the Road 41
5 An Ideal Husband 55
6 Travelling Solo 67
7 A New Partner 77
8 London and the Literary Life 91
9 Chautauqua 107
10 The Final Tour 121
Epilogue: The Happy Hunting Grounds 139

Chronology of
E. Pauline Johnson (1861-1913) 143
Sources Consulted 163
Index 167

Brant Historical Society

Pauline's father, Chief George Henry Martin Johnson, *Teyonnhehkewea*, is a well-educated man descended from a long line of Mohawk chiefs.

When Emily Susanna Howells, an upper middle class white woman, marries George Johnson, both native and white people disapprove.

Brant Historical Society

Emily and George Johnson's fourth and youngest child is named Emily for her mother and Pauline for the only sister of Napoleon, her father's idol.

1

The Star of the Show

It is just seven-thirty on Saturday, January 16, 1892, but every seat in the art gallery of Toronto's Academy of Music has already been taken for the city's first ever "Literary Evening." It's not scheduled to begin until eight, and the event's sponsors, the Young Men's Liberal Club of Ontario, are rushing to find chairs for the stream of people still arriving on this snowy night. Everybody who is anybody in the city – or who hopes to become somebody – wants to be seen here because it is the "in" thing this season to be known as a patron of the arts. And tonight some of Canada's finest authors will be reading from their prose works or reciting their poetry.

When at last enough chairs have been found and everyone has stood at attention to sing the national anthem, Frank Yeigh, the club's president, steps to centre stage to introduce the first author, an aging poet who is known to her public as "Fidelis." Her very long poem is read to the audience by the Reverend McDonnell. Afterwards the audience claps politely. Author Wilfred W. Campbell follows with another long poem and an even longer prose piece. They clap with a little less enthusiasm. But when William Duow Lighthall takes centre stage to read a whole chapter from his latest history, the drone of his voice and the warmth of the room begin putting people to sleep. The applause is half-hearted when he eventually finishes.

Frank Yeigh is very anxious as he walks onto the stage to make the next introduction. An ambitious man, he's been counting on this literary evening to make his name in society as well as in politics, but he knows he has a disaster on his hands, unless...*unless* the woman who is next on his list can save the show. "Ladies and gentlemen, I am honoured to introduce our next author, a friend from my childhood years in Brantford. You have read her poems in *The Globe* and in that fine journal *The Week*. She is the daughter of the late Chief George Johnson of the Six Nations. Ladies and gentlemen, I give you Miss E. Pauline Johnson reciting her poem, 'A Cry from an Indian Wife.'"

In the audience, wives poke their drowsing husbands, urging them to pay attention. This is the author they have all come to see – that *Mohawk Indian girl who writes poems*. They sit forward, expecting some black-haired, barefoot maiden, some savage creature dressed in feathers and buckskin. Instead, the woman who crosses demurely to stand at centre stage is dressed in a pale grey silk gown, fashionably trimmed with cut-steel bead fringes. Her hair is not black; it is dark brown, and the newly installed electric stage lighting brings out reddish highlights in her elegant coiffure. Standing with her hands clasped behind her back, she looks calm and composed as she waits for the audience to be quiet again.

Yet Pauline Johnson is very nervous tonight. While she waited backstage, she was trembling so much with stage fright that she could feel the bead fringe on her skirt rattling against her knees. She knows that tonight she must have the audience's full attention because the poem she has chosen to recite concerns the Riel Rebellion of 1885, still a controversial political topic at this time. Her poem challenges the conviction generally held in Ontario that the government had been right to confiscate the land claimed by Riel and his followers. In spite of her nervousness, her voice is clear and strong as she begins.

My forest brave, my Red-skin love, farewell,
We may not meet tomorrow; who can tell
What mighty ills befall our little band,
Or what you'll suffer from the white man's hand?

The audience listens in complete silence as her poem demands how they would react if soldiers came to take *their* lands by force. Pauline's voice rises passionately.

They but forget we Indians owned the land
From ocean unto ocean; that they stand

Upon a soil that centuries agone
Was our sole kingdom and our right alone.
They never think how they would feel today
If some great nation came from far away,
Wresting their country from their hapless braves,
Giving what they gave us – but wars and graves.

When she reaches the final lines, the hot, stuffy air of the Academy is electric with emotion.

Go forth, nor bend to greed of white man's hands,
By right, by birth, we Indians own these lands,
Though starved, crushed, plundered, lies our nation low…
Perhaps the white man's God has willed it so.

Pauline bows her head; there is no applause, not even a whimper of protest from the audience. She is sure she has offended them all and has already turned to flee from the stage when suddenly they are on their feet, clapping wildly and shouting "Bravo!" and "Encore!" Astonished, she turns back to them, bows again, then walks quickly from the stage. The applause goes on and on. She can't believe it! *They liked her poem!* In the wings, a smiling Yeigh is waiting for her, grateful that she has saved his literary evening and his reputation. He leads her back to centre stage, and when the applause at last dies down, he promises the audience that Pauline will recite again after the intermission. "You're the star of my show!" he tells her as he escorts her backstage again. This is all overwhelming for Pauline because, although she is thirty-two years old, this is the first time she has ever recited one of her poems in public.

For her encore, Pauline Johnson recites "As Red Men Die," a poem she based on a legend told by her grandfather, Chief John "Smoke" Johnson, who was perhaps the most important influence on her life. Known as the "Mohawk Warbler" for the poetry and music of his language in debates, he had been appointed speaker of the Six Nations Senate in 1842. He shared his vast knowledge of his people's history and ceremony with the young Pauline and told her of his long ago exploits on the battlefield beside Joseph Brant against the Americans in the War of Independence, and beside British troops in the War of 1812. He died aged ninety-four in 1886. "As Red Men Die" retells his story of a Mohawk forebear who chose death by walking on a bed of live coals rather than accept life as a slave. The people in the audience are thrilled by the warrior's bravery, and when Pauline finishes, they are on their feet applauding wildly again.

At the close of the evening, Pauline walks the short distance to her hotel with Yeigh and his fiancée, Kate Westlake. Barely able to contain her excitement over the events of the evening, Pauline recounts how, just before leaving the Academy, a man who fought Riel in 1885 had come backstage to speak to her. "He said, 'When I heard you recite that poem, I never felt so ashamed in my life of the part I took in it!' "

"Do you realize," Yeigh says, "that you could make a career of reciting?"

"On the stage?" Pauline laughs. "Mother would never approve. Do you remember what my parents said when I told them I wanted to be an actress?"

In Canada in the 1890s no decent parents would ever give permission for their sons or daughters to go on stage. Although it is socially correct to attend the theatre, the actors who perform there are not the sort that nice people ask home to tea because their offstage lives are considered unwholesome, even downright scandalous. There are exceptions to the rule, of course. Famous actors touring with Shakespeare's plays are considered socially acceptable because Shakespeare is believed to be morally uplifting, and celebrated stage beauties can always count on being welcomed into the drawing rooms of the wealthy and the titled. But most actors are still classed with thieves and pickpockets.

Pauline's parents simply will not hear of her ambition to be an actress. The Johnsons, after all, have gone through many difficult years establishing their social position. On her father's side, Pauline is descended from a Mohawk Indian family that includes a long line of chiefs. Pauline's mother, Emily Susannah Howells, comes from an upper middle class English Quaker background and counts the American novelist W.D. Howells among her cousins. But when George Henry Martin Johnson and Emily Howells married in 1853, there was opposition from both families, and they suffered the humiliation of crowds clamouring to see them on their wedding day as if they were circus freaks. While many white men had taken native Indian wives in colonial times, it was unheard-of for a white woman of Emily's class to marry an Indian even if he was a cultured and well educated chief.

Chief Johnson's reaction to this insulting treatment was to build a fine mansion for his bride; called

Chiefswood, it stood on the bank of the Grand River on the edge of the Six Nations Reserve. In this beautiful house, Emily Johnson, morbidly sensitive to public opinion, raised her four children by the strictest rules of conduct, teaching them never to lose control of their emotions and to remain dignified and well-mannered at all times.

Pauline, the youngest of the family, was educated by governesses until at fourteen she was sent to the Brantford Collegiate. Since her parents had forbidden her to become an actress, after graduation she stayed at home writing poems and stories, occasionally earning a few dollars when one of them was accepted by a publisher.

She would probably have remained home writing until the right man came along to marry her, but in 1884, when her father died from complications after a bout of the streptococcal infection, erysipelas, the family discovered they could no longer afford to live in Chiefswood. Pauline – who was then twenty-three – and her mother and older sister, Eva, moved to a small house in the town of Brantford. Pauline's two older brothers, Henry in Toronto and Allen in Hamilton, were employed by insurance companies, and Eva promptly took a job as a bookkeeper in the office of the Indian superintendent in Brantford.

In these circumstances Pauline, keeping house for their mother, can see only one possible future for herself: writing and getting married. She has high expectations of the man she will marry: he must be as gallant, courageous, and intelligent as her father, but because she equally admires the British from whom her mother is descended, and with whom the Mohawks were traditionally allied, he must also be British. In the white community of Brantford, however, young men with these qualifications are not eager to marry a woman who is so proudly determined that everyone should know she is a Mohawk Indian. As a consequence, though she is charming, beautiful, talented, and popular, nine years have gone by without an acceptable offer of marriage. The years have not been entirely wasted: she has published a number of poems and a few stories. But since she is still unmarried, she knows she must find a way to support herself soon because her mother is getting old and the family's pension will cease when the old lady dies. The question is: will her family approve of Yeigh's idea?

"Recitalists," Yeigh is quick to point out, "are not in the same social class as actors." In fact, recitalists are in a profession running parallel to theatre and using the same facilities, although they call their stage a "platform," and are often referred to as "platform performers" to make it perfectly clear that they are not actors. They are generally preachers or teachers or writers, and their lectures and readings are intended to spread culture, not entertain. However, they sometimes show lantern slides to illustrate their talks, an element of entertainment that encourages attendance. "Your family couldn't possibly object!" Yeigh tells Pauline.

But Pauline is remembering that her brothers and sister and mother had all found excuses not to attend on this night, as though afraid that she might disgrace them. And she knows that as a recitalist she will have to behave with the ultimate in decorum if she is not to lose her respectability.

"Let me be your manager," Yeigh says enthusiastically, "and you'll be the star of your own show every night! Trust me, I can book you into the best halls in Ottawa and right across Ontario." Then, suddenly inspired, he adds, "You could fix yourself up in Indian togs!"

Yeigh is not taking much risk. He knows she will be a success, not just because of her performance this night, but because she is a born actress. In spite of her parents' refusal to allow her to become a professional, Pauline has had stage experience. With her brothers and sister she took part in family theatricals at Chiefswood, generally performing scenes from Shakespeare before an audience of family and friends, and later she starred in plays at the Brantford Collegiate, where Yeigh had seen her perform. After the family's move to Brantford, she joined the Dramatic Society there and frequently took lead roles, even performing in nearby Hamilton. With her natural flair for comedy, she gained a reputation as a clever comedienne and was soon garnering favourable newspaper reviews. Her mother had raised no objections because the dramatic society's membership was composed of absolutely respectable amateur actors.Yeigh knows he won't be wasting his time as her manager.

"I'll think about it," Pauline tells Yeigh.

"Think about this," Yeigh says. "A year on the platform – maybe two at the most – and you could earn enough money to take your poems to London to have them published in a book!"

Now he has hit a nerve. Publishing a book of her poems is the thing that Pauline wants most. It would establish her name as a poet and make selling future poems that much easier. When she mounts the stairs to her hotel room, she is thinking seriously about Yeigh's idea, but she returns to Brantford the next day without giving him an answer.

On Monday morning the literary page of the Toronto *Globe* complains about the long-winded recitalists at Saturday night's Literary Evening, but they are full of praise for Pauline. "Miss E. Pauline Johnson's may be said to have been the pleasantest contribution of the evening.... It was like the voice of the nations that once possessed this country, who have wasted away before our civilization, speaking through this cultured, gifted, soft-voiced descendent."

As Pauline reads the review to her mother and sister, Emily Johnson smiles with pride. Since her husband's death eight years ago, Emily has consoled herself with the company of her younger daughter, partly because Pauline is so like her father in looks and vivacious personality, and partly because Pauline's poems seem to be saying the things that are in Emily's own heart. When Pauline tells her of Yeigh's plans for a recital tour, Emily is torn between her desire to keep her daughter home beside her and her eagerness for Pauline's verses to become famous. Overriding both is her anxiety that a career on the recital platform will not be considered entirely respectable. What will society think of a young woman trouping around the countryside unchaperoned? But at last she gives her cautious approval. "Just until you have earned enough to take your poems to London, of course." Pauline agrees.

Pauline's sister, however, strongly disapproves of the proposed recital tour. Although Eva is grudgingly impressed by her sister's success in publishing her poems and the accolades she has received for her debut at the Literary Evening, she is firmly opposed to Pauline making a career of it in case it reflects badly on the family. Underlying her opposition, however, is her resentment that their mother obviously prefers her younger sister. A frail child subject to constant colds and earaches, Pauline was pampered more than the other Johnson children, and when she showed an early aptitude for composing poems and stories, she quickly became everyone's favourite. Eva has always been envious of the attention Pauline is given, but because she has been taught never to lose control of her emotions and never to express her anger, she disguised her resentment by fussing over Pauline, hoping to win her mother's approval in that way. Now once again she is forced to stifle her objections in the face of her mother's approval of Pauline's plans.

Two days later Pauline telegraphs Frank Yeigh,

Dear Yeigh-Man:
Mother approves. When do we begin?

She signs it, "Your Star."

Brant Historical Society

Reassured by her manager that recitalists are in a higher social class than actors, Pauline becomes a touring performer to earn her living.

Brant Historical Society

Paddling her canoe "Wildcat" gives Pauline such pleasure that she is inspired to write her soon-to-be famous poem "The Song My Paddle Sings."

2

The Aboriginal Voice

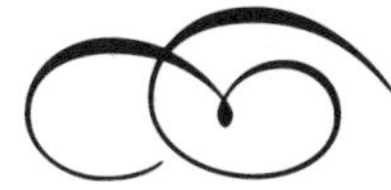

Just one week after Pauline's appearance at Yeigh's Literary Evening, advertisements in Toronto's newspapers announce that Miss E. Pauline Johnson will recite in Toronto's Association Hall on Friday, February 19. Yeigh has wasted no time launching her tour; he knows that the public will soon forget about his star if he waits too long. And he doesn't want to give her time to change her mind.

Since Yeigh's father was a newspaperman and he also worked on newspapers before turning to politics, he has friends on most of the local papers, so it's a simple matter for him to arrange publicity for the recital. The result of his efforts is a spate of news items about the Mohawk poet. On February 13 the *Globe* reports that "Charles G.D. Roberts, the Canadian poet, says of Miss Johnson: 'She is the aboriginal voice of Canada by blood as well as by taste and special trend of her gifts.'" A few days later it is announced that Pauline has completed a new poem especially for this performance, and it will be published in *Toronto Saturday Night* immediately after the recital.

But it will take more than the preparation of a single poem to make a recital because audiences expect a full two hours of entertainment – not including an intermission. Yeigh has hired two soloists – Maggie Bar Fenwick and Fred Warrington – to take up a half hour of the evening, not, however, as an opening act, but to perform at the end of the first half of the program in order to give Pauline's voice a rest. But this still means that Pauline will have to recite for at least one and a half hours. With Yeigh's guidance, she chooses the best of all the poems she has written in the previous ten years and rehearses them in front of her mother and sister. Unlike most of the currently popular recitalists, she has never had elocution lessons, so she hasn't learned the exaggerated facial expressions and gestures that they use. Instead, to charge her poems with every ounce of their dramatic impact, she will rely on her extremely musical voice, clear enunciation, and remarkable ability to project her voice to the farthest corner of a hall.

She poses for publicity photographs, and Yeigh distributes them to the newspapers. She buys a steamer trunk to carry the gowns she will wear on stage and a valise to carry her everyday apparel. Although most fashionable ladies hire a dressmaker to make their evening gowns, Pauline, unable to afford a seamstress, sews her own stage costumes and refurbishes old gowns, sometimes with the help of her sister. As each gown will be worn at least thirty times in the next two years, packed and unpacked, sponged and pressed and worn again, they must all be extremely serviceable. Sheer fabrics and easily crushed ruffles and trimmings are out, but since Pauline must look fashionable and elegant on stage, she uses heavy satins and velvets decorated with braid and enhanced with lace capelets and feather boas.

Pauline's guide in creating her stage wardrobe is a glamourous Belgian actress named Mlle. Rhea, whom she met in 1885 when her brother Allen took her backstage after a road company performance of *The Widow*. Rhea, the star of the play, was known more for her costumes than her acting ability, and on this occasion she was wearing the gown that the Queen of Holland had worn for her coronation – rose-embroidered gold satin with a four-yard-long black satin train embroidered with a bird of paradise. Pauline was enchanted by both the actress and the gown, and Rhea invited her to tea the next day. With Emily Johnson's wary approval, they became good friends, and Rhea's autographed photo took pride of place in the Johnson family's front parlour.

On February 19 there is a full house at Association Hall. The curtains part and Frank Yeigh steps confidently onto a stage adorned only with a small table crowned with a bowl of pink roses. As Yeigh begins his lengthy introduction, explaining how Pauline acquired her Mohawk name, *Tekahionwake*, from her great-grandfather, then enlarging on her illustrious Mohawk heritage, he can feel the impatience in the audience. These people want to hear Pauline herself, not him. They've come to listen to more legends of heroic Mohawks courageously facing death.

But Pauline, with Yeigh's guidance, is about to take a calculated risk. Instead of beginning the program dramatically with poetry drenched in blood, she has chosen to begin quietly with her new poem, the lyrical "The Song My Paddle Sings," a poem that arose naturally out of her lifelong love of canoeing. As a very small child she had been sickly, prone to colds and bronchitis, but by the time she was eleven, her health had improved enough that her brothers taught her how to paddle a canoe. She soon knew every shallow and rapid on the Grand River and paddled her little canoe "Wildcat" as if she had been born on the water. Fortunately, in the intervening years canoeing has become a fashionable recreation for both men and women, and dozens of canoe clubs have sprung up all over Ontario. Pauline knows that "The Song My Paddle Sings" will be popular because it captures the rhythm and joy of paddling and the sweep of the river as it "rolls in its rocky bed."

The applause is prolonged when she finally steps onto the stage in a pale cream-coloured silk gown with a small train. When the house is hushed, she begins:

West wind, blow from your prairie nest
Blow from the mountains, blow from the west.
The sail is idle, the sailor too;
O! Wind of the west, we wait for you.

Blow! Blow!
I have wooed you so,
But never a favour you bestow,
You rock your cradle the hills between,
But scorn to notice my white lateen.

She pauses. The audience, already caught up in the rhythm of the poem, leans closer. She looks out over their heads. The seconds stretch on and on. She takes a rose from the bowl and tears a petal from it. Then another petal. To the audience she looks perfectly composed. In fact, Pauline is suffering an attack of stage fright and has actually forgotten the words to her own poem. *Oh, what on earth is Yeigh-man going to say to me?* she thinks. Finally she returns the rose to the bowl.

"Will the audience permit me to recite a different selection?" she asks.

There is momentary silence, then polite assenting applause. When it dies, she begins to recite "In the Shadows," a paddling poem that she wrote in 1886. It is received enthusiastically, but the audience gets what it has really come for with her next selection, "The Avenger." Without making a single melodramatic hand movement, she leaves them shivering as her compelling voice spins the chilling tale of a Mohawk warrior whose brother has been treacherously slain by a Cherokee. It ends with the Mohawk addressing the killer:

> "Last night, thou lent'st the knife unto my brother,
> Come I now, oh Cherokee, to give thy bloody
> weapon back to thee!"

An evil curse, a flash of steel, a leap,
A thrust above the heart, well-aimed and deep,
Plunged to the very hilt in blood
While Vengeance gloating yells, "The Debt is paid!"

It is not until the second half of the program that Pauline feels confident enough to return to "The Song My Paddle Sings," and this time she remembers every word. She ends the program with a dramatic reading of one of her prose pieces called "Indian Medicine Men and their Magic," which is scheduled to be published in *The Dominion Illustrated* in April 1892. The audience loves it, and next day the *Globe* announces, "Miss E. Pauline Johnson scored another triumph at Association Hall on Friday evening!"

Toronto Saturday Night's reviewer is the only one to make mention of her difficulty remembering her lines, but he is full of praise for the rest of the recital of "her own magnificent poetry."

> ...She has a face surprisingly mobile, a good presence, and is thus equipped for the expression of emotions. Many of the poems she recited were of strong dramatic quality, and it was strikingly apparent that the great acceptability of her work was due to the fact that she really felt and knew how to portray the emotions that her lines described.... Scorn, contempt and sarcasm were admirably expressed in her rendition.... In the lapse of memory which happened during the recitation of "The Song My Paddle Sings," she

> showed admirable coolness in appreciation of the position in which she stood toward her audience. It may not have spoken for the quality of Miss Johnson's poetry for it is sufficiently well known that her magnetism and her aptitude for public appearance alone make the hearer wish to see more of her....

Within a month of this initial performance, Pauline is on tour. Wherever she performs – even in the backwoods – Yeigh has made sure that people have already heard of her. Posters advertising her recitals have been hung in each town weeks before she gets there, but there is good word-of-mouth advertising too, recommending her from one town to the next. The owners of the concert halls also print up "dodgers," handouts that pass on the comments of audiences in other towns. But while most of them contain reports about her fine recitals, far too many of them promote her concert by stressing the fact that she is a curiosity – an Indian woman who writes and recites poetry.

This attitude isn't a surprise to Pauline. The members of her family have never been completely accepted by either white or native society. Pauline's father, who spoke Onondaga and Oneida as well as Mohawk and English, was employed as a translator while he was still in school, first by a missionary of the Presbyterian church and later by the government. From this job he rose to become government agent or "warden" on the Six Nations Reserve. When he was elected chief, there was an outcry from tribal members and the Six Nations Senate because his work for the

British government could lead to a conflict of interest. But since offices among the Mohawks are passed down through the matriarchal line, his mother was able to force his acceptance as chief. When Chief Johnson married a white woman, once again there was disapproval and ostracism, this time from both native and white communities.

Now, instead of trying to make Pauline acceptable to her white audiences by playing down her native heritage, Yeigh decides to capitalize on it, and with Pauline's approval he begins billing her as "The Mohawk Princess." It is a phoney title because although Pauline is legally Mohawk on her father's side, he was not a full-blooded Mohawk; his maternal grandmother was a white woman, kidnapped by the Mohawks and raised as one of their own. And Pauline's mother is white. As well, the term "princess" is strictly a white man's appellation and cannot be applied to the daughter of an elected head. But for advertising purposes it is a stroke of pure genius!

In order to dress to suit her new title, in the fall of 1892 Pauline "fixes herself up in Indian togs," as Yeigh has suggested. The costume she designs is a mid-calf-length dress of buckskin lined with red flannel and fringed at the hemline. But when she has one sleeve sewn into place, she shows the costume to her sister.

"What do you think, Eva?" she asks, modeling it. "Somehow I think the sleeves are going to be too... elaborate."

Eva stares at the dress for a few minutes. The lone right sleeve is formed of a strip of beaded buckskin, one end attached to the shoulder of the dress, the other to a band at the wrist. Hanging from both edges of this strip are long buckskin fringes. Eva nods in agreement. Two sleeves like this will be simply too much. "Why not make one sleeve like that and use skins for the other one?"

Pauline gathers up a couple of the rabbit pelts that she has planned to hang from the belt of her dress and drapes them over her upper arm. "Yes," she says. "That's perfect!"

She finishes the dress with a round neck trimmed with a fringe of buckskin and decorated with a dozen silver brooches made from hammered coins. Later, when the Hudson's Bay Company presents her with twelve matched ermine tails, she will fasten them around the neck of her dress with these brooches. At her waist she wears her father's hunting knife, several wampum belts, and a Huron scalp she inherited from her grandfather. With the dress she wears buckskin leggings and mocassins. The red woollen cloak which hangs from one shoulder is made from the blanket that was spread on the ground for Prince Arthur, Duke of Connaught, when he was made an honourary chief of the Six Nations in 1868. Since then it has served as a cover for the Johnson's piano. For the rest of her recital career she will wear this costume for the "Indian portion" of each of her performances, a fashionable ball gown for the other half.

For the next year and a half Pauline tours all over Ontario. For the first six months she plays the larger towns, mostly on Friday and Saturday nights; in October, Yeigh, who runs her tour from Toronto, begins booking her to recite in a different settlement every night. She travels during the day by train and horse carriage to her next stop, performs that evening, takes a room in the local hotel for the night, and in the morning begins her journey to the next town. After five or six days of this routine, Yeigh leaves a gap of a few days in her schedule to give her time to go home to Brantford, rest, repair her costumes, and write more poems and short stories. By May 1893 she has given 125 recitals in more than fifty small-town church halls and schoolhouses.

Pauline's only companions are the performers Yeigh finds to share her programs, and at first these change from night to night. In the cities he has no difficulty finding first-class pianists, violinists, and singers to perform with her as word quickly gets around that she can attract a full house. In the small towns, however, Yeigh is forced to hire "local talent," usually without being able to audition them. As a result, Pauline frequently finds herself dealing with stage-struck singers who have never before faced an audience or pianists who have forgotten their music.

For someone else, this might be an achingly lonely life, but Pauline, although fun-loving and gregarious, has always kept people at a slight distance, and as a result, has never known truly intimate friendships. As a child she earned the nickname "Proudy" from the other children on the reserve because of the aloofness that her mother taught her to strive for. When she attended the Brantford Collegiate, she boarded with family friends – an aged man and his two spinster daughters – in a house where the other boarders were all young men. Her mother was not worried for her safety; she knew that her daughter would follow her parting advice to the letter: "Never under any circumstances allow a gentleman to take liberties with you; never allow him to lay a finger on your hand. It is only ill-bred girls that allow boys to touch them. It is not aristocratic." Pauline, anxious not to be considered ill-bred, carries these rules over into her relationships with women as well; she is cordial and friendly but discourages any sign of approaching intimacy.

Very few are tempted to break through this wall of reserve, making it possible for Pauline to travel unchaperoned throughout Ontario giving recitals. She does have men friends, but she sets the boundaries of their relationships with her. When the artist George Reid takes her to see Ernest Thompson Seton's wolf painting, *Awaited in Vain*, she seizes both the up-and-coming artist's hands in hers. "I know that we are kin," she tells Seton. "I am a Mohawk of the Wolf Clan, and that picture shows that you must be a wolf spirit come back in human form." Later she sends him a silver talisman in the shape of a wolf, but it is friendship she offers, nothing more. They correspond for the next twenty years but meet in person again only a half-dozen more times.

Her reputation of unassailable propriety also makes it possible for Yeigh to partner her onstage in November 1892 with a young Englishman named Owen Alexander Smily. At twenty-three years of age, Smily is already a veteran of five years on stage in British music halls, generally as a comedian. He is an accomplished pianist and is quite capable of making up lyrics on the spot. A ventriloquist and impersonator, he can switch from Scottish to Irish to Cockney to Yankee accents whenever he chooses. He even does a skit where he pretends to play the bagpipes and imitates their drone.

When Yeigh first suggests sharing her stage with Smily, Pauline's initial concern is for her reputation, but Yeigh reassures her that the partnership will be a formal business relationship only. Their private lives on the road will be entirely separate. As a result, they will be able to travel unchaperoned for months at a time without stirring a breath of scandal. She also raises her concern about appearing on the same stage as a comedian; her poems are, after all, very serious and dramatic. Fortunately, she has a sparkling sense of humour, and when Smily makes her laugh, she is won over.

Their first appearance together is for a return engagement at Toronto's Association Hall on November 25, 1892. Smily is welcomed with applause and laughter, but he is clever enough not to attempt to outshine the star of the show. Much more experienced now, Pauline glides onto the stage with confidence and mesmerizes her audience. But there is something more than just experience in her performance now because Smily, who doubles as an elocution teacher in the off-season, has been giving her lessons. The newspaper critics are eloquent in their praise; Pauline doesn't let them in on her secret.

During the following spring Yeigh still teams Pauline with local talent on a number of occasions, but by the summer of 1893 Pauline and Smily have become a permanent team. Now, instead of Smily performing once just before halftime as Pauline's other backup acts have done, the two performers alternate on stage, with a number of selections from Smily, followed by several poems from Pauline. Smily's acts come straight from his music hall days with sketches called "Major McStynger's Mechanical Arm" and "How Billy Atkins Won the Battle of Waterloo" and nonsense pieces where he performs at the piano with "Music in Three Flats" and "Music and the Mind." Pauline still electrifies the audience with her dramatic monologues based on Indian legends and woos them with her lyrics, but from watching Smily perform, she begins adding little jokes or bits of doggerel to her own routines, usually in reference to some local event or institution.

The partnership works out so well that they begin collaborating on short skits, and for the finale of their joint program, the two perform a play that Pauline has based on her short story, "A Red Girl's Reasoning," published in the February 1893 issue of *The Dominion Illustrated*. Smily plays Captain Charles Fielding, a young Scottish immigrant, who is stationed at a remote trading post. There he meets Christy, a beautiful girl whose mother is a native, her father a white man. Fielding and Christy marry, and he takes her to Ottawa where she inadvertently tells a society hostess that her parents were only married "Indian fashion." Fielding is mortified and tells her that she has disgraced him. She leaves, and when he finds her again, she refuses to return to him because "Neither church, nor law, nor even love can make a slave of a red girl." The play is a sensation with audiences.

Her partnership with Smily provides Pauline with one extra dividend: now, whenever she is ill, there is no need to cancel a scheduled performance and forfeit the door receipts. Instead, Smily simply takes over the whole program for that evening. And unfortunately, Pauline is frequently ill with bouts of bronchitis and laryngitis, the afflictions that have plagued her since childhood.

In August 1893, before Pauline and Smily set off to tour the Maritimes together, Pauline returns to Brantford for a brief holiday with her mother. Together the two women travel to Brophy's Point in the Thousand Islands, where Pauline is to be the special guest of the Cataraqui Canoe Club at the annual camping and canoeing meet of the American Canoe Association. Each club is required to entertain at the nightly campfire, and Pauline is asked to be the Cataraqui's headliner. When their turn comes, the Cataraqui singers, supported by an "orchestra" of banjos and mandolins, serenade the campers until, with everyone comfortably mellow, they announce in chorus: "Miss...Pauline...Johnson...will...now...re-e-e-e-cite!"

Out of the shadows and into the firelight glides Pauline in her buckskin costume. In a voice filled with bitterness and suffering, she begins:

My forest brave, my Red-skin love, farewell,
We may not meet tomorrow; who can tell
What mighty ills befall our little band,
Or what you'll suffer from the white man's hand?

Sitting around the campfire, the young men and women shiver with something more than the chill of the night air. Pauline is called back again and again for encores, and when she recites "The Song My Paddle Sings," many of them join in because they already know her poem by heart.

For Pauline there is another attraction at this canoeing meet: Harry O'Brien. Four years younger than Pauline, he is a Toronto lawyer and commodore of the Muskoka Lakes Canoe Association. And although she is at this meet as the guest of the Cataraqui Club, it is Harry O'Brien that she cheers for in the regatta.

Brant Historical Society

Armed with letters of introduction and her hard-earned savings, Pauline sails to England to search for fame and a publisher for her poetry.

HE **MANAGEMENT,** in presenting to the English public, **TEKAHIONWAKE, MISS PAULINE JOHNSON,** The Canadian Iroquois Indian Poet Entertainer, feel confident she will repeat the many successes she has won in her native land. Many Poet-Entertainers have appeared in the mother country, but it is safe to say that none so gifted or unique as this daughter of the great Iroquois tribe of Indians that remained true to the Crown during the early French and American wars in Canada. She holds with Campbell, Roberts, and Carman the reputation of being the most popular writer, and her entertainments in the larger Canadian cities have always been largely attended, and not only were the social but the artistic events of the season.

Pauline is promoted as *Tekahionwake*, the Mohawk Princess. She dines with British and Canadian aristocracy and hobnobs with London's artistic set.

3

The Toast of London

In January 1894, exactly two years after making her decision to tour as a recitalist, Pauline Johnson is ready to make her expedition to London to find a publisher for her first book of poetry. She has been warned that this will be a long and expensive process: first she must establish her reputation as a recitalist and poet in London's entertainment business; then she must find a reputable publisher who likes her poetry enough to undertake the job; and finally, she must supervise the editing of the manuscript and proofing of the galleys. The funds she has saved should pay for her passage and perhaps as much as three or four months in London, but only if she spends with care. However, two years of earning her own living have allowed

Pauline to indulge her extravagant tastes. It is now habit for her to stay in the best hotels, dine in the best restaurants, and wear the finest kid gloves and boots; it is going to be difficult for her to live on a strict budget in a city with so many enticements.

Throughout the spring of 1894 while she continues touring with Owen Smily, Pauline acquires letters of introduction to influential people in London's literary and social set. Among them, she will be looking for "patrons" to sponsor her, people who will arrange for her to recite in public in order to establish her reputation, people who will introduce her to a publisher.

Her method of obtaining letters from government members and officials is simple and not very subtle: she writes each one a letter gently reminding him that the Indian Act makes all native people wards of the state. The implication is that each member of government is therefore her surrogate father and should care about her welfare as a father would. Her artless request generally ensures that the recipient will provide her with at least one letter of introduction to some important person. Her tactics change only slightly when she begs letters from men in the literary world: she begins by telling them how much she admires their writing and wishes to emulate them; then she makes her request. It helps that most of those to whom she sends these begging letters have seen her perform and know that she is a very talented poet and recitalist – as well as a very beautiful woman. None are offended by her requests. In fact, they are flattered because in these days before emancipated womanhood, it is expected that a lady will look for aid and protection from men – first to fathers, husbands, and brothers, then to men of power and influence. The men are only pleased that such a talented, beautiful woman has chosen to turn to them.

As Pauline prepares for her trip, her most difficult task is reviewing her poems to select those to take with her. These will be the poems by which posterity will remember her. She will take all the paddling songs, of course, because by this time canoeing is popular in England as well. And all her lyrical descriptions of pastoral scenes must go with her, too. But the most important ones, as far as she is concerned, are the dramatic monologues that retell Indian legends, and she has no idea how an English publisher will react to them. She will take them anyway and try to persuade the publisher of their value.

Pauline will be going to London alone. Owen Smily has no wish to return to England, and Frank Yeigh has fulfilled his promise to her; now his own career must take precedence. On Thursday, April 26, the good people of Brantford hold a bon voyage party for Pauline in the main reception hall of Kerby House, the town's best hotel. Wearing a mauve gown with a cream-coloured "waist" and matching hat, she stands alongside her mother, her sister Eva, and her brother Allen to greet the guests with the three society hostesses who have organized the affair. Then, one after the other, the town's leading politicians, clergy, and other prominent citizens deliver speeches in praise of Pauline's talents. The mayor, coming last, presents her with a purse full of English sovereigns that have been donated by the people of Brantford.

The next morning a group of friends sees her off at the Grand Trunk Railway station. Eva and Allen board the train as well to travel with her as far as Harrisburg, Pennsylvania; then she continues on to New York alone to board the Cunard steamship *Etruria*.

After five seasick days Pauline arrives on the cold grey docks of Liverpool in the drizzling rain and catches the train for London. But there are no hansom cabs meeting the trains at Euston station because the cabbies are all on strike, and Pauline has to carry her hand luggage on board an omnibus. It takes her to 25 Portland Road, Holland Park West, the elegant house where she has rented a small "studio" flat for the duration of her stay.

In spite of this dismal beginning to her great adventure, Pauline is not dismayed. London, even in the rain, holds an air of excitement. Its buildings are covered with centuries of grime and soot, its air is polluted, its narrow streets are crowded with horse-drawn carriages and filthy with garbage, but it is the hub of civilization and culture in this final decade of the century.

Pauline begins her search for patrons two days later. She delivers each of her letters of introduction by hand and in return generally receives an invitation to attend an "at home," usually during the following week. At these afternoon events Pauline meets all the elegant people of London's social set. Because she is introduced to them as *Tekahionwake*, the Mohawk Princess, they regard her as exotic royalty. Almost immediately she is in demand for evening recitals in the private homes of duchesses and countesses. They are even more impressed when she performs wearing her buckskin costume. Within weeks she becomes the toast of the London season and promptly receives more invitations to recite than she can possibly perform.

At one of her recitals, Arthur, Duke of Connaught, is in the audience, and at the end of her performance, he sends an aide to ask Pauline what became of the red blanket he had knelt on during the ceremony on the Grand River Reserve. "Will you tell His Highness," Pauline responds, "that the mantle that I wear was once honoured by his feet." She doesn't tell him that it also served as the family's piano covering.

None of this hobnobbing with the rich and famous fazes Pauline. Her mother always insisted on impeccable manners and ladylike behaviour at all times so Pauline is quite at home in these grand drawing-rooms, and her father taught her to regard all people – native and white – as equals. At Chiefswood there had been a constant stream of people coming to consult with him, including ordinary people from the reserve lands and high government officials. As a child she had watched as he officiated at the ceremony making the Duke of Connaught a chief of the Six Nations people. She was twenty-three in 1884 when the Johnsons were visited by the governor general, Lord Dufferin, and his lady; five years later she had stood beside her parents to curtsy when they greeted his successor, the Marquis of Lorne, and his wife, Princess Louise. And since she began her recital career, she has met and recited for Canada's prime minister and most of his cabinet. Now in London it is only the butlers and footmen in their fancy uniforms and gold braid and stiff manners who intimidate her because they look down their noses at everyone!

In early May, still searching for a patron, Pauline carries a letter of introduction from the Earl of Aberdeen, Canada's governor general, to Lord Ripon, former viceroy of India and now Britain's colonial secretary. Ripon is ill and cannot see her, but a month later when he is recovered she is taken to meet him and his lady by Sir Charles Tupper, Canada's high commissioner in London. The next afternoon, at tea with her ladyship, arrangements are made for Pauline to recite at the Ripons' next major dinner party.

At dinner she is seated between Lord Ripon and the deputy speaker of the House of Commons and enjoys herself immensely discussing politics. "My grandfather," she tells them, "was speaker of the Six Nations Confederacy." When they express ignorance about the confederacy, she explains that it was founded by Hiawatha in the fifteenth century and that it gradually welded together six nations who had warred on each other for centuries, ruining the economies of all of them. "Hiawatha," she says, "was the only statesman who ever solved the problems of perfect government and perfect economy." They are impressed that a mere woman knows so much about government and even more impressed with the recital she gives in the drawing-room after dinner. The Ripons, congratulating themselves for having discovered her, decide to be Pauline's patrons.

In the meantime, she continues her search for a publisher, first seeking out someone to type all her handwritten poems so they will appear more impressive. She looks for "some worthy girl who has a mother and a little brother to support. I did not go near an agency bureau," she reports later, "but spent five days hunting up my worthy girl. She said her charge was a guinea – I had expected to pay two – I gave her one and a half. But when I looked at the work – Oh, it was awful! I do not know how long it took me to correct it. There were words spelled wrong, whole lines left out, dreadful punctuation and other things you can imagine!" But with time running out, she does not have it typed again.

Although many of her letters of introduction are to people in the arts and in literature, none of them are addressed to publishers, so she has to rely on one of her literary contacts to direct her to one. In early June, with a letter of introduction in hand from Professor Clark of Trinity University, she goes to visit Clement Scott, the critic who has dictated the dramatic tastes of London society for two decades.

Scott is at work on a book of his own, and when Pauline arrives, his housekeeper says he cannot be disturbed.

"But I *must* see him," Pauline says.

The housekeeper relents. "But only for a minute," and she leads Pauline to Scott's study.

"Well?" he demands, scowling.

Pauline is convinced that she will have to deal with the man through his vanity, and she turns as if to leave. "I'm afraid to come in," she tells him.

"Come back here!" he roars. "What are you afraid of?"

Pauline approaches him cautiously. "I'm always afraid of a man who can make one or ruin one with a stroke of his pen."

Flattered, Scott responds just as she expects him to. He looks over the manuscript, then scribbles a note to his friend John Lane, one of the partners in The Bodley Head, the most prestigious publisher of poetry in England.

Lane takes the manuscript from her, then bellows, "What do you mean by getting this copy typewritten?"

"Why," Pauline replies nervously, "I thought it was necessary."

"No," he snaps, "it is not! I never take a book for publication without the expectation that my author will be great, and how would *this* look in the British Museum labelled, 'Original Manuscript of Miss Johnson's first book'?"

But Lane accepts her submission. "I would not dare," he says, "refuse anything that Clement Scott recommended."

He now sends the manuscript to three well-known poetry critics, John Davidson, Percy White, and Richard le Gallienne, for their opinions on its worth, and as a result it is not until the end of June that the decision is made. The Bodley Head will publish her poetry. But first Lane assigns John Davidson the tasks of deciding which poems will be included in the book and of editing the final product.

Davidson, an acid-tongued Scotsman, is not gentle in his criticisms of Pauline's work, consigning some of her verses to the trash pile without apology. "The Avenger" he dismisses as too melodramatic, but to her relief he likes seven of her other "Indian poems," including "A Cry from an Indian Wife" and "As Red Men Die," although he does insist on making improvements in all of them. Pauline submits to this ruthless attack on her work with horror at first, then quickly grows to admire the man and to learn from him.

Meanwhile, between recitals she continues to attend social functions among the titled and those from the artistic set. One of these events is a musical evening at the home of the artist Sir Frederic Leighton at 12 Holland Park Road. Here in the main hall, designed to represent the banqueting room of a Moorish palace, Leighton entertains against an exotic background of massed tropical plants and ornaments collected on his travels in the Middle East.

She goes to bohemian tea parties at John Lane's rooms just around the corner from his publishing house. There she meets everyone from would-be poets to notorious authors like Oscar Wilde and William Watson. She celebrates Dominion Day at a party at the Westminster Palace Hotel. Organized by Sir Charles Tupper, it is a splendid affair attended by all the Canadians living in London. It is all a far cry from Ontario and the small settlements where she has performed for the past two years.

But soon it is mid-July, and even though she has been paid for all her drawing-room recitals, Pauline's funds are rapidly running out after just ten weeks in London. Her money has gone to what she considers good causes, however. Some has subsidized the publishing of her book because Lane is unwilling to pay all the costs for a relatively unknown "colonial" writer. Some has gone for clothes. In Westbourne Grove, dressmakers have made four ball gowns for her in the latest London fashions, far more elegant than anything she has owned before, gowns she will wear at future recitals. She has spent money on tickets for the theatre, which she has attended whenever she wasn't performing herself; she has seen the greatest actresses of the age – Eleanora Duse, Ellen Terry, and Sarah Bernhardt – and learned much by watching their acting techniques.

But now the London "season" is over. There are no more drawing-room entertainments to give because society has moved to country homes for the summer, and entertainment there is limited to tennis and garden parties. Left behind in London where the weather has turned miserably wet and windy, Pauline suffers from a sore throat and bouts of laryngitis as she works with Davidson to complete the revision of her manuscript. When at last it is ready for printing, she realizes that she cannot afford to stay here and wait for it to come from the presses. She has the comfort of knowing that it will be published simultaneously by the Bodley Head in England, the Copp, Clark Company in Toronto, and Lamson Wolffe and Company in Boston.

She takes the train to Liverpool and boards ship for home. At the rail as the ship pulls away from the pier, Pauline finds herself standing next to a talkative American tourist with a litany of complaints about the service she has received in England. "And when I asked for ice water," she tells Pauline, "they looked at me as if I was some North American savage!"

"Do you know," Pauline says quietly, "that's just the way they looked at me."

When the woman seems puzzled by this remark, Pauline explains that she is one of those "North American savages."

"Oh," says the woman, not at all abashed by her *faux pas*, "was your father one of those real wild red Indians?"

"Yes," Pauline responds.

"Why, excuse me, dear," says the woman, "but you don't look a bit like that!"

Pauline takes a moment to recover from this one, then she asks, "Was your father a real white man?"

"Why, 'course he was, dear," the lady answers.

"Well, excuse me, but I'm equally surprised," Pauline remarks and leaves her standing at the rail. Below in her cabin a few minutes later Pauline decides she will be very glad to be home.

McMaster University

Throughout her career, Pauline will wear her bear claw jewellery and her buckskin dress with its two different sleeves for the "Indian" half of each performance.

4

On the Road

On Thursday, July 26, 1894, Pauline is hardly inside the door of her mother's home in Brantford when reporters come calling. "What happened in London?" they ask. "Did you find a publisher? What are your future plans?"

"In that charming manner, peculiarly her own," the Brantford *Expositor* reports, "she chatted most pleasantly of her experiences in the great city of London." According to the newspaper, Pauline then explained that her next tour would begin the following week in Orillia and follow the CPR to the west coast. "I don't know whether I'll go south to San Francisco or not, but I'll return to commence the Ontario season in October."

All this is very bad news for Emily Johnson. She had hoped Pauline was coming home to live quietly with her in Brantford and resume her writing life. But Pauline explains that the trip to London and subsidizing the publishing of her book have taken all her savings. For now, she must perform in order to publicize the book and recoup some of that money. But one day, Pauline promises, she will be so famous that she can afford to stay home and write. What she doesn't tell her mother is that she has always planned to continue touring after the trip to London. She loves performing, and from her first success on stage she has never had any intention of giving it up.

Four days later, she sets off for Toronto with her valise and the steamer trunk that contains her four new ball gowns and her Indian costume. In Toronto she stays at the Rossin Hotel, and the next day teams up again with Owen Smily. Together they meet with Ernest Shipman, their new manager. Unlike Yeigh, whose own career now leaves him no time to book halls and arrange publicity for them, Shipman is in business as a theatrical agent, and because he has many clients, he won't be concentrating all his energies on them. They will have to resolve any problems that arise on tour themselves.

As they work so well together, the partners are pleased to be reunited, and since neither has been farther west than Sudbury, they are eager to get started. But before they catch the train for Orillia, they make one more stop in Toronto, this time at the offices of the *Globe* newspaper. When they leave, Smily has a contract to write a travelogue of their adventures on the trip west, and Pauline has been engaged to write a poem for each of the major towns enroute. This tour will be a money-maker for both of them.

By Yeigh's standards, Shipman has arranged a very sedate tour for them. They will play only the well-established settlements along the rail line or close to it, a total of thirty-five performances over two months. Although it is impossible for Shipman to guarantee them first-class accommodation aboard trains since they will be stopping off for performances at least every second day, they will seldom have to take their chances on local transportation. And because they will play only large settlements, the hotels should be reasonably decent. But the best part of this modest tour is that by the time they return to Toronto they will know if the wild west is ready for recitalists.

The train takes them northwest to Sudbury with stopovers for a dozen performances along the way. Shipman has guaranteed that they will play to full houses at each of these stops by advertising that both performers are appearing "direct from London" – though this is stretching the truth as far as Smily is concerned. From Sudbury they take the branch line to Sault Ste. Marie. Although their schedule leaves little time for fun, after their performance here, Pauline persuades a Chippewa native to take her canoeing through the rapids. She arrives back from the adventure, soaked with spray, just as the train is pulling out to return them to Sudbury.

From there it is northwest again to arrive at Rat Portage (Kenora) on August 23, the next day doubling back to play Port Arthur. It is here Pauline becomes enthralled with western Canada. To her long-time canoeing friend Harry O'Brien she writes:

> Ah! There are no such airs as these in England, no such skies, no such forest scents and wild sweet perfumes. These August days are gorgeous. The atmosphere is rife with amethyst, amber and opal tints, parented by the far off bush fires and the thin north air. The sun lays like a ball of blood, and oh! the stillness, the silence, the magnitude of this country impresses me as it never has before. I cannot tell you how I love my Canada, or how infinitely dearer my native soil is to me since I started on this long trip.

Sweltering in the late-summer heat, the partners undertake a week of one-night stands to packed auditoriums in Morden, Boissevain, Souris, Carman, Manitou, and West Selkirk. They travel between these towns by horse and buggy in "a great blistering breeze like a breath from a bake oven," which leaves them both covered in a thick layer of grey dust. In Winnipeg they perform four times with a different sponsor every night: the Winnipeg Grace Church, the Rover Bicycle Club, the Church of Zion, and the North Presbyterian Congregation. The church recitals strain Smily's repertoire somewhat because he can't entertain with his rowdier pieces; instead he enacts tragic monologues like "The Death Watch of the Bastille." But the people of Winnipeg are so welcoming that Smily decides it is part of a conspiracy to prevent tourists from travelling farther west. "It is hard to believe that such geniality and kindness from comparative strangers cannot be without an object. It seems too good to be true."

After Winnipeg, the stopovers are farther apart. On September 11 they perform at Brandon; two days later they are on stage in Medicine Hat. It is here that Pauline receives a telegram from her mother. Henry Beverly Johnson, Pauline's elder brother, is dead. Only forty years of age, he died of a heart attack on the street in Columbia, Pennsylvania, where he was on an organizing and inspection tour for his new employer, the Anglo-American Loan Investment Company. Pauline is too far from Brantford to be home in time for his funeral. She goes on stage to recite, her heart heavy. "No one knew he was ill," she writes to her friend O'Brien.

> It was so sudden, and the shock to me is awful. And so I go on night after night before the public – for when one is under signed contract, they may not have a heart. It was worst while he lay dead, and I in gay gowns and with laughter on my face and tears in my heart went on and on – the mere doll of the people and a slave to money....

For Pauline, what makes Henry's death even sadder is that he was alone. Long before his death he ceased to regard Brantford as his home and after 1888 even stopped joining the family there for Christmas. He blamed his mother for the fact that he felt unable to marry, and he told Pauline that their mother should have talked of the nobility and beauty of love and the honour of marriage instead of choking off their human tendencies. "We'll all be waifs and strays one day," he had told her. "Not one of us will ever marry."

After a performance at Pincher Creek on September 15, Pauline and Smily take a horse and buggy ride back to Lethbridge to perform. On the way they spot a pair of wolves feasting on the remains of a cow, and Smily, inspired to play the frontier hero, whips out his pistol and fires at them. Undisturbed, the wolves continue their dinner. "If I had aimed at the sun," he writes later, "the wolves might have had more occasion to examine their insurance policies." But Pauline, for whom the wolf represents a far more romantic tradition, immediately takes out pencil and paper to jot down notes for a poem that begins "Like a grey shadow lurking in the light/ He ventures forth along the edge of night;..."

On September 18 they drive back to Fort Macleod for a recital at the North-West Mounted Police (NWMP) outpost established there in 1874. While waiting for curtain time, the two performers watch Indian pony races. "The riders dispense with saddle and ride barebacked (both horse and jockey)," writes Smily. "An article resembling an apron is the only habit of the latter. When the word is given to go, they go! It is the very opposite of an eastern race. There the onlookers do all the yelling, but the uproar of the spectators at Macleod was as the snap of a toy pistol to the bang of a rifle compared with the sustained war-whoop of that mob of naked Indians as they whirled past. What a bonanza a dozen of them would be scattered through the audience in some of those towns where it is considered vulgar to applaud!"

They play Calgary for two nights, then climb aboard the CPR again for Banff, Canada's new national park. To Pauline's intense disappointment, all the mountains are shrouded in a snowstorm. Although both performers have heavy colds by this time, they give their recital, then move on to Golden where they perform on September 22. This is their last stop before the coast, where they are greeted with a downpour that lasts for their entire stay.

Their Vancouver recital audience is "not as large as the merits of the performance demanded," reports the Vancouver *Daily World*, "but as large as could be expected on such a bad night." The reviewer commends Pauline's performance, then adds, "Mr. Smily is a clever entertainer and his character sketches were, every one of them, sidesplitters!"

After staying at the CPR's expensive Hotel Vancouver and the Empress in Victoria, Pauline decides to economize in Nanaimo by booking rooms for them both in the Royal Hotel. It is only the fact that Smily balks when he sees this rundown waterfront hotel and insists on staying at a better one across the street that saves their lives because that night the Royal and the entire block in which it is centred burns down, cremating three of the hotel's guests and seriously injuring another score. Pauline has learned her lesson: she will never willingly choose a second best hotel again.

After this blazing finale Pauline and Smily head east once more with a sheaf of enthusiastic reviews from newspaper critics. After a week's rest they are on a tour of Ontario towns when, on December 15, the *Globe* publishes a full-page article called "There and Back" by Owen Smily and Pauline Johnson. Smily's prose is lighthearted and the readers' response is very favourable, but Pauline's poems, many of them also intended to be humorous, are roundly condemned by many readers. She is accused of "masquerading as a poetess" and "descending to the use of slang!" Fortunately, loyal fans ride to her rescue with letters-to-the-editor in her defence, although none of them seem to realize that she was trying to match the humour in Smily's prose.

In July 1895 Pauline's book of poetry is finally released by the publishers. *The White Wampum* is only eighty-eight pages long and contains just thirty-six poems. It is, however, an impressive looking volume with a red-brown cover decorated with a design, by artist E.H. New, of a ceremonial hatchet and a wampum belt engraved above Pauline's adopted name, *Tekahionwake*. Each poem begins on its own page of heavy cream-coloured stock.

In Canada the critics' responses to the book are all enthusiastic and once more elevate Pauline Johnson to celebrity status in her homeland. In Britain, however, reviews are mixed. Some critics commend her lyrics and turn thumbs down on her Indian poems; others are enthusiastic about the monologues while condemning her lyrical poems. *The Guardian*'s reviewer, unaware that she is native, writes: "The idea of posing as an Indian bard cannot be counted among her happiest inspirations." A week later the same newspaper, by now aware of their reviewer's gaff, prints another review, this one approving all her poems.

Meanwhile, by the time the book is released, Pauline and Smily have already completed a second western tour, this time visiting the smaller settlements away from the rail line. Their itinerary includes a recital at Cannington Manor, forty miles (sixty-four kilometres) south of Moosomin, Saskatchewan. A unique settlement organized by Captain Edward Pierce, it is peopled by upper class English families who indulge in regular fox hunts and spend their evenings in literary and artistic pursuits. Here the Beckton brothers entertain Pauline and Smily at Didsbury, their twenty-two room mansion, and the partners perform that evening in the Cannington Town Hall to an audience in full evening dress.

In the fall Pauline and Smily head east to play one-night stands in the Maritime provinces. The next year follows the same pattern with a tour of Ontario sandwiched between one of the Prairies and British Columbia and one of the Maritimes. In 1897 they go south of the border to play Michigan, Indiana, Ohio, Illinois, and Iowa, then they head for western Canada again.

Although audiences in the big cities are sophisticated enough to accept the transition Pauline makes from the word music of poems like "The Song My Paddle Sings" to her romantic tales of native heroism, in small settlements she has to resort to presenting two distinct characters, not just two different costumes. First she appears onstage as a lady of culture in her London ball gown; after the intermission the fiery

Indian maiden dressed in buckskin takes her place. And just to make sure the audience has made the transition with her, she adds offstage war whoops before she delivers poems such as "The Avenger."

As the years go by, she learns more of Smily's tricks for pleasing audiences. She composes bits of doggerel to celebrate local characters and events, she invents humorous stage business – often with Smily as the straight man – and she even makes jokes. When her friend Harry O'Brien accuses her of debasing herself by these devices, she admits she plays to the public but has to do it if she is to be successful. She writes him:

> More than all things I hate and despise brain debasement, literary "pot-boiling," and yet I have done, will do these things, though I sneer at my own littleness in so doing.... You thought me more of a true poet, more the child of inspirations than I have proved to be. The reasons for my actions in this matter? Well, the reason is that the public will not listen to lyrics, will not appreciate real poetry, will in fact not have me as an entertainer if I give them nothing but rhythm, cadence, beauty, thought.... Ye gods, how I hate their laughter at times, when such laughter is called forth by some of my brainless lines and business. I could do so much better if they would let me. I have had dreams of educating the vulgar taste to poetry, not action. I will do it some time, when this hard, cold, soulless reason for bending to their approval ceases to exist.

Pauline has become a realist. In this period before the turn of the century, there are no more than a dozen cities in all of Canada – most of them in the east – that have large enough "opera houses" – the term used at this time for concert halls – and a consistent enough theatre-going public to merit regular stops on the itineraries of travelling theatrical companies. The entertainment tastes of the population of these cities is therefore somewhat sophisticated, and Pauline could entertain an audience here with a whole program of "lyrics" because the social elite regard her offerings as culture. However, most of her recitals are delivered to unsophisticated small town audiences who have only been lured to the local opera house because the advertising posters promise more sensational fare. The bits of doggerel and jokes that she adds simply help to keep them in their seats to the end of the show.

In the large cities Shipman either rents a hall for their recital and hires someone to promote it or he arranges for a recital sponsor, usually a church or club or lodge. Renting a hall has the potential to give the pair a larger return because after the shares for the hall owner, the promoter, and their agent are paid from the door receipts, what remains is theirs. Sponsoring groups give them only a percentage of the admissions, although frequently they also "entertain" the performers, that is, provide overnight accommodation in their members' homes.

Giving recitals in small towns takes more stamina. The performers are at the mercy of the owner of the local hall or "opera house" and must rely on him to advertise the event well enough to bring in an audience from the surrounding farms and ranches. He will take his share of the admissions first; they will get what's left. And if he hasn't promoted the recital well, their share may be nothing. When there is no hall in the community, they rent the local schoolhouse, the church, the Masonic chambers, a warehouse, or even the dining room of the local boarding house. After the show, they are generally "entertained" because most of these little settlements don't boast a hotel. But sometimes they are reduced to waiting on the train station platform after the show to catch the train as it roars through in the early hours of the morning.

Since many of the people in farm communities have never attended a live performance before, Pauline and Smily are sometimes faced with dead silence throughout their show. No one in the audience is sure if it is correct to applaud, and they know for certain they shouldn't laugh because "culture" isn't a laughing matter. In other audiences the farmers make loud comments from the moment the curtain goes up. Whole families attend, including the youngest infants, whose lung power is sometimes enough to drown out the performers. Schoolboys heckle and, when they get bored with that, throw apples and turnips onto the stage.

Pauline faces one other problem in the small communities that Smily does not have to suffer: although they welcome the entertainment she brings them, many of the farm wives – uneducated but morally upright women – consider her a "stage actress" with all that the term implies. They therefore regard her as a potentially evil influence on their children and menfolk. When they see her in the flesh, what wins them over is her aura of purity and aloofness, and in the end they are persuaded to mother her instead.

Should Pauline ever want to be an immoral woman, there are plenty of opportunities with all the lonely wifeless men populating these settlements, but she has an enormous stake in maintaining her exemplary reputation. The slightest breath of scandal will bar her from the front parlours of Canada's upper class, and if she succeeds in returning to England, from the drawing-rooms of her titled friends. But even more importantly, she still hopes to marry into the upper levels of Anglo-Canadian society, and she knows that gentlemen do not marry loose women.

Charles Robert Lumley Drayton fulfilled all Pauline requirements for a husband, but their engagement outraged his parents and their Toronto social circle.

B.C. Archives

WINNIPEG THEATRE FRIDAY FEBRUARY 3

E. PAULINE JOHNSON RECITAL

PART I.

1. Reading . . . "Wolverine" . . . *Johnson*
   E. PAULINE JOHNSON
2. Song . . . "When All the World Is Fair" . . . *Cowen*
   MISS MERRIELLE PATTON
3. Reading . . . "The Riders of the Plains" (With introductory remarks.) . . . *Johnson*
   E. PAULINE JOHNSON
4. Ballad . . . "The Three Maids" . . . *Anon*
   MR. C. W. HANDSCOMB
5. Reading . . . Selected . . . *Johnson*
   E. PAULINE JOHNSON
6. Song . . . "The Lass With the Delicate Air" . . . *Old English*
   MISS MERRIELLE PATTON
7. Reading . . . "The Legend of Qu'Appelle" . . . *Johnson*
   E. PAULINE JOHNSON
8. Song . . . "Idle Words" . . . *Adams*
   MISS MERRIELLE PATTON

PART II.

9. Ballad . . . Selected . . .
   MR. C. W. HANDSCOMB
10. Readings (Two dog stories) . . . (a) "Beyond the Blue" (b) "Lumberman's Xmas" . . . *Johnson*
    E. PAULINE JOHNSON
11. Song . . . "The Butterfly Courtship" . . . *Hardelot*
    MISS MERRIELLE PATTON
12. Reading . . . "A Case of Flirtation" . . . *Johnson*
    E. PAULINE JOHNSON

NOTE—All Miss Johnson's numbers are of her own composition.

The Piano used for these performances is from the Mason & Risch Piano Co.

The Winnipeg Theatre Orchestra can be engaged for receptions and balls For terms apply to S. L. Barrowclough, director.

Mason & Risch Pianos are used in all leading Canadian Theatres

McMaster University

After a year in which she was often ill and in which her mother died, Pauline's Winnipeg recital receives savage reviews from the critics.

5

An Ideal Husband

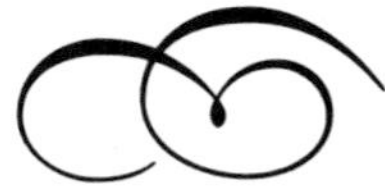

The partnership between Pauline Johnson and Owen Smily ends in the fall of 1897. Except for the two-and-a-half months of Pauline's visit to London, they have worked together continuously for five years. Now their business relationship has been undermined by jealousy; Smily is tired of playing backup for Pauline, and she is unwilling to share top billing. He is making plans to headline a show of his own.

Their last recital together is in rural Ontario in late November. There is no press announcement that this is the end, nor is there any gossip about their disagreements; Pauline always handles differences of opinion with ladylike discretion, and Smily is well aware that disclosure will damage his gentlemanly image.

Pauline has much to be grateful to Smily for. The high quality of his performances has enhanced their show, while his tutoring has made her own stage appearances more polished, confident, and truly professional. Whenever she has had one of her increasingly frequent attacks of bronchitis or laryngitis, Smily has taken over the show, leaving her to make a mere token appearance. He has been good company on their long journeys, and his presence has discouraged unwanted advances from overly enthusiastic admirers. But their relationship is now so strained that after they part, Pauline never speaks of him again.

After three weeks of solo recitals in Ontario and a brief trip home to Brantford for Christmas with her mother, Pauline catches the westbound train to keep a performance date in Winnipeg's new Grand Opera House on December 29. She and Smily have used this city as their base for the past three years of travel in western Canada and the central states. For the last two of those years, Pauline has rented a permanent room for herself in the Manitoba Hotel. It has become her home-away-from-home, and in return for favouring their city, the people of Winnipeg have taken her to their hearts.

It is five months since she performed in Winnipeg, and when the tickets for her recital go on sale, they are sold out within two days. Three of those tickets are bought by men who will make a difference to Pauline's future plans. One of them is purchased by Charlie Handscombe, the drama critic for the *Manitoba Free Press* and Pauline's good friend. The second goes to the young man who will sit beside him,

J. Walter McRaye – born Walter Jackson McCrea in 1876. McRaye is just twenty-one but he has already survived eighteen months touring as an actor, entertainer, and monologuist. Now he is unemployed and hoping that an introduction to Pauline by his friend Handscombe will catapult him into the role just vacated by Owen Smily.

The third ticket belongs to Charles Robert Lumley Drayton. At twenty-five, he is already assistant inspector for the Canada Permanent Loan Company. Working out of that company's Winnipeg offices, he has spent three years travelling by train and horse carriage throughout the Prairies and British Columbia and is now recognized as one of the foremost property evaluators in the country. He and Pauline met sometime during the summer of 1897 and he promptly fell under her spell. He is not the first man to pay court to her, but he is the first to fulfil all her requirements for a husband: he is as handsome, gallant, courageous, and intelligent as her father, and he is also British.

The opening act on this gala evening is a young violinist named Ernest du Domaine and his piano accompanist, Albert Betourmay, but they get scant attention because this audience has come to see and hear Pauline. They greet her appearance onstage with a standing ovation, then applaud wildly after each recitation. At the end of the evening they are on their feet again, demanding encores, but although she is usually generous, on this night she merely "bows her acknowledgements" and leaves the stage smiling.

Handscombe and McRaye hurry backstage to intercept her, but Pauline is already in her dressing room. Drayton is guarding the door. He is taking her for a late supper in the dining room of the Clarendon Hotel. Pauline, always gracious to the press, invites Handscombe and McRaye to join the supper party – much to Drayton's disappointment. Before the night is over Pauline has hired McRaye to be her backup for a week of one-night stands in southern Manitoba in early January.

J. Walter McRaye's forte is the performance of the poems of Dr. William Henry Drummond, which have just been published in a collection called *The Habitant*. From it, McRaye selects "The Wreck of the *Julie Plante*" and "Leetle Bateese," which are written in Drummond's version of Quebec patois. As well, McRaye recites selections from Shakespeare and Victor Hugo. A tiny man with a large ego, he is not a great performer, but he is always cheerful and optimistic and has learned to be unflappable when problems arise on the road. Thus he makes an ideal companion for Pauline's quick tour of southern Manitoba.

After the tour, McRaye heads south to try his luck in the Dakotas, and Pauline returns to Winnipeg. On arrival she sends a note around to the three local papers, outlining her schedule for the next year. She will give a recital in Winnipeg on January 18, followed by two months of engagements on the Prairies, after which she intends to return to Ontario for a short tour before going to New York. There she will be making arrangements for the publication of a book of her short stories. An American tour will come next and in September she will embark for a season of recitals in Australia.

But the only part of this itinerary that actually happens as outlined is the January 18 recital; a sore throat and severe laryngitis cause the cancellation of her Prairie bookings, and she remains in residence at the Manitoba Hotel to recuperate. Then to everyone's surprise, on January 25 she issues another press release, this time to announce her engagement to Charles Drayton. The marriage will take place in September, the newspapers report, after Pauline returns from New York and her American tour.

Although Drayton has all the basic requirements to be Pauline's ideal husband, they really have little in common. She is profligate with money; Drayton, the financier, is careful to the point of miserliness. She is headstrong and determined to have her own way; he believes in obedience and duty. She sees the romance in this vast country; he sees its dollar value. But the most crucial differences are in their backgrounds. Drayton is the second son of a former officer in His Majesty's 16th Rifles, a man who is now a lecturer and examiner at Osgoode Hall law school and a King's Counsel. Philip Drayton is a stern, unimaginative man with absolute control of his two sons. In 1888 he took Charles's elder brother, Henry, into his office to study law, then prodded him up the ladder so that Henry is now assistant solicitor for the city of Toronto. By apprenticing Charles to a finance company, he expected that his second son also would attain high office.

When the news of Charles's engagement arrives in Toronto, Philip Drayton is outraged. Marriage to a woman like Pauline Johnson is not part of his plans for his son. In the first place, he does not see any distinction between recitalists and actresses; even though Pauline has performed for royalty and has been welcomed in high society in Canada and England, she is not acceptable in *his* social circle. Furthermore, he expects his sons to marry women who will give them heirs. And while Pauline looks far younger than her years and is still referred to as a girl by reporters and adoring fans, she is thirty-six years of age, past her best years for child-bearing. But as far as Drayton Sr. is concerned, the worst thing about Pauline is that she loudly proclaims her native heritage; to Philip Drayton this is nothing to be proud of. He immediately fires off a letter to his son forbidding the marriage.

Many of Pauline's friends and admirers are also appalled by news of her engagement but for far different reasons. The society columnist for the Brantford *Courier* expresses the town's sentiments when she writes:

> That her rare accomplishments and pleasing personality should win many bids in the matrimonial market was to be expected, but Miss Johnson was enthroned by her genius far above the commonplace of life and getting married is such an ordinary thing to do that it was the last thing expected of her. "She will never be the same," said one. "She will lose her individuality."
>
> "Not a bit of it," I said. "An individuality like hers is not easily lost. Mr. Drayton is the one to be pitied in this respect. He will go

through life as the husband of Pauline Johnson, the Indian poetess."

However, Pauline sees neither the letter from Philip Drayton nor the reported views of Brantfordites because, having recovered from her laryngitis, she leaves Winnipeg on January 28 to fulfil her rescheduled Prairie recital engagements. But arriving in Regina in blizzard conditions on February 20, she is handed a telegram from her brother Allen. Their mother is dying and has asked to see her youngest child one more time.

Pauline cancels the remainder of her tour and catches the next eastbound train. Again and again as enormous snowdrifts sweep over the tracks, the train is forced to a halt. It is three days before it reaches Winnipeg and there's another six-hour delay before it heads east again with the storm still howling. Five days later Pauline finally arrives in Brantford. Three-quarters of an hour after she reaches her mother's bedside, Emily Johnson dies.

Hundreds of people attend the funeral and witness Emily's burial beside her husband in the old Mohawk Cemetery. Her obituary in the Toronto *Globe* recalls "the astonishment with which society received the news of the engagement and subsequent marriage of the popular and much admired Miss Emily Howells to a full-blooded Indian, Chief Johnson by name. That this unusual marriage should have turned out most happily is only another proof of the fact that what everybody says is not necessarily true." Among the hundreds of bouquets and "floral emblems" that cover the grave are cut flowers sent from Charles Drayton in

Winnipeg and violets from Mrs. Philip Drayton of Toronto. Pauline, who has by this time been made aware of Drayton Sr.'s opposition, is heartened to think that they have one ally in the Drayton family.

Nursing yet another cold and throat infection, Pauline stays on at the family home with Eva in order to settle their mother's affairs. Without Emily acting as a buffer between her two daughters, tensions run high between them, and no decisions have been made concerning the estate when Pauline returns to the recital platform at the end of March. For the next two months she fulfils her bookings on the circuit between Toronto, Ottawa, and Sudbury, then heads for New York state to give a series of recitals for the Indian Association. By the end of May she is back in Brantford with another throat infection. This time she remains in bed under Eva's dubious care for nearly a month.

But there is still more sadness ahead. On July 9 Charles Drayton's mother dies; she is just fifty-one. Pauline goes to Toronto for the funeral. When she and her fiancé find no opportunity to discuss their future together, she returns to Brantford the next day. During the next two weeks the Johnson family furnishings are divided, and Pauline sends her share for storage at the home of her cousin Kate Washington in Hamilton. On the last day of July the two sisters leave the family home for the final time. They are barely speaking to one another. Pauline's official address is now the Manitoba Hotel in Winnipeg.

She has not given up on marrying Charles Drayton, although his father remains implacably opposed. As soon as she arrives in Winnipeg on August

6, she issues a press release, and the *Manitoba Morning Free Press* dutifully reports that she will be embarking immediately on a new tour of the northwest "after which her marriage takes place in Winnipeg where she will permanently reside."

But once again before her tour can begin, she becomes ill, and the doctor who is called to her hotel room announces that this time she is suffering from rheumatic fever. After three weeks she is well enough to be moved to the home of friends who nurse her back to health. It is September 26 before she returns to the recital platform.

Having dispensed with Shipman's services when she announced her plans to marry Drayton, Pauline signs up with a new agent. Thomas E. Cornyn manages a string of actors from offices in Toronto and Winnipeg and runs a road show called the Bijou Comedy Company. Cornyn's first fall tour for her takes her to more than fifty small prairie settlements, and although she has played equally gruelling schedules in her days with Smily, this time she must provide the entire evening of entertainment by herself. She cannot afford to hire local talent to take over a portion of her program because her illnesses have depleted her savings; she is living now from recital to recital. Even brief holidays are a luxury, and she no longer has the option of quitting the recital circuit and returning home to Brantford and a writing career.

As well, she is seriously depressed. A year of repeated illnesses, the death of her mother, and the dawning realization that Charles Drayton is unlikely to challenge his father's edict have all left their mark. She has lost weight, her beautiful complexion has suffered, and the vitality that sparked her performances is gone. She is not a great success on tour, and when she returns to Winnipeg to give a recital on February 3, 1899, she is savagely critiqued by the city's reviewers for the very first time. The next day as she leaves town for the west, she does not announce a new date for her wedding. Instead she tells reporters that she will not return to Winnipeg until after an extended tour of Australia.

On February 8, 1899, the Manitoba Hotel burns to the ground, consuming a trunkful of possessions she has left there in storage. This event marks the end of Pauline Johnson's love affair with Winnipeg.

Brant Historical Society

Pauline's share of the rent paid by the tenants of her childhood home, Chiefswood, provides her with money when she is desperate.

McMaster University

Pauline's domineering older sister, Eva, disapproves of her extravagance and of her new stage partner and manager, J. Walter McRaye.

6

Travelling Solo

In February 1899 Pauline Johnson's tour route takes her west once again into southern Alberta, then north to Edmonton, back to Calgary, and across the Rockies to the coast. The newspaper reviews of her shows range from lukewarm to scathing. After complaining that her poetry has become boring, the Vancouver *Province*'s critic writes:

> Miss Johnson showed a fault which she seemed to have slipped into...that of relying on gesture and forceful delivery for effects of vehemence rather than by more intimate study, obtaining the result through intellectual means and aiding her own cause by the suggestion of reserve.

Two qualities that have made Pauline's performances consistently superior to those of other recitalists have been her subtle gestures and beautifully nuanced, expressive voice. Now, tired and lacking energy, she has taken an easier route by using the standard tricks of the professional elocutionist – a loud voice and much arm-waving – to keep her audience's attention. The effect – as demonstrated by the *Province*'s review – has been disastrous.

To compound her problems in the Vancouver recital, Pauline has introduced a new monologue, cobbled together in hotel rooms and on trains. Eventually revised and named "Mrs. Stewart's Five O'Clock Tea," it is the comic tale in verse of a newcomer to Ottawa hosting her first society reception. Pauline plays all the characters, including a mining promoter, a down-at-heel vicar, a pompous railway director, and a child who is supposed to recite for the party but forgets her poem. But this new piece is far too long and rambling, and the audience squirms and loses interest. If Smily had still been with her, she would have rehearsed it in front of him and he would have helped shape and tighten it; now she is writer, director, producer, and performer of her own shows and has to wait to read the critics' reports to know how well she is doing. And these critics are not kind and sympathetic to her problems.

But Pauline has never been one to give up in the face of criticism, and the Vancouver review acts as a wake-up call. She puts the tea-party sketch aside for reworking, and in Cranbrook in the east Kootenays, three weeks after the Vancouver recital, the reviewer commends her for being "graceful in her movements, pleasing in her tone, and charming in appearance" and for holding her audience "with perfect ease."

By late May she has worked her way back to Calgary. That summer she plays the Dakotas and Minnesota and by fall is on the Prairies again, touring the area that will soon be known as Saskatchewan. On November 16 in Qu'Appelle she draws an enthusiastic audience of more than two hundred people, a remarkable turnout in such a small settlement. Just before Christmas she returns to Winnipeg to perform at the Grand Opera House. The program she gives is polished and confident, a one-woman variety show in which she tells anecdotes about her adventures on the road, introduces new poems written on her travels, and even revives "Mrs. Stewart's Five O'clock Tea" in a new and more compact version. It is a success this time.

She spends Christmas 1899 in Winnipeg with friends, and before she leaves the city in early January, she has one last meeting with Charles Drayton. He asks to be released from his engagement to her so that he can marry someone else. Although breach-of-promise suits are common in this period, Pauline does not consider this an option; an aristocrat doesn't stoop to such tactics. She releases him without argument, her emotions carefully hidden.

As the year 1900 begins she is busy giving benefit concerts for the Canadian regiments setting off to fight beside the British against the Boers in South Africa. Organized by patriotic citizens, these concerts raise funds for the troops' medical services, personal comforts, and widows' pensions, none of which are paid for by government. At the Massey Hall concerts in which Pauline is starred, she introduces two of her newest poems, the patriotic "Canadian Born" and "Riders of the Plains." The critics are ecstatic.

To Pauline the time now seems ripe for her long-delayed Australian tour; her health has improved, and she has learned how to stage a balanced one-woman show that rivets her audiences' attention. She decides on June as her departure date. There is only one thing lacking: the money to get her to Australia. Although she has toured without a break for ten months, her bank account is almost empty. She has, however, worked out a plan to replenish it.

At the end of January she travels to Ottawa to give a number of recitals and while there calls on the Minister of the Interior, Clifford Sifton. She targets him because his ministry includes Indian Affairs, and his bureaucrats are responsible for collecting the rent from the Chiefswood tenants and distributing it to the heirs – Pauline, Eva, and Allen Johnson. Pauline's request to him is simple: will he arrange to give her an advance of five hundred dollars on her share of the rent money? If he agrees, she will not receive rent money again for the next three-and-one-half years, but Pauline is convinced that this is a small price to pay; five hundred dollars will be enough to buy a first class passage to Australia and pay her hotel bills for a lengthy tour of that continent. And perhaps it will make her fortune. To her relief, Sifton approves her request and assures her that she need only write him if she ever needs help again. By mid-February the money is in her hands.

As has become her habit, Pauline does not tell her brother or sister what she has done. She knows Eva will rage about Pauline's extravagance and attempt to force her to give the money back. With luck, however, Eva and Allen won't learn about the advance until summer, when Pauline intends to be far, far away.

In the meantime, Pauline continues her recitals in Ontario. Then in early June her name appears in the Halifax *Herald* alongside the news that she will not be going to Australia that month, after all. Instead she will tour Nova Scotia. This announcement is made by her brand new manager, a handsome New Yorker named Charles Wurz. In a press interview he explains grandly that Pauline will be appearing in two dozen Nova Scotia towns before leaving for the United States where she will give recitals in a number of key cities. He has, he tells reporters, decided to delay her extended tour of Australia until the fall, and afterwards she will tour Britain as well.

Only days later the Halifax *Herald* begins printing a series of enormous – and very expensive – advertisements for her upcoming Nova Scotia recitals. According to the ads, the tour will begin in Dartmouth on June 14, followed by a gala performance the next night in Halifax to be attended by patrons that include the lieutenant-governor, the premier, several admirals, and an archbishop. In a town where she has always drawn sell-out houses on the strength of a five-line note in newspaper entertainment columns, these ads are unnecessary. But Wurz is playing the big-time promoter – with Pauline's money.

On the evening of June 14 Pauline plays to a capacity crowd in Dartmouth. It is pouring rain when she leaves the theatre, but she sets out in an open buggy for Halifax to meet Wurz and arrives at the Halifax Hotel soaked to the skin. Within hours the hotel management is forced to call a doctor, who diagnoses "acute rheumatism," another name for rheumatic fever. This time it is twelve days before Pauline is able to rise from bed, and when she does, she discovers her tour has been cancelled and Wurz has disappeared – apparently taking with him the remainder of her five hundred dollars.

A month later she is well enough to leave the hotel. Acting as her own agent, she reschedules some of the cancelled dates in order to pay her hotel and medical bills. By mid-August she is performing in Prince Edward Island, by late September in Newfoundland, and by November in New Brunswick. Although she is not fully recovered from her latest illness, she gives remarkable performances to adoring audiences. But the constant touring is taking a heavy toll of her energies. In one five-day period in late November she gives a recital in Fredericton, then travels by horse and carriage to Woodstock only to learn that her recital there has been poorly advertised and has to be cancelled. She goes on from there by rail to perform in St. Stephen, then begins the long trip back to Fredericton for a second recital scheduled for November 24. At McAdam Junction, where she is to change trains, she is informed that there will be a delay because of snow on the tracks. As she sits in the station crocheting Christmas gifts, another woman waiting for the same train offers to share the lunch she has brought. Recognizing Pauline, she asks questions about her life and is appalled to learn of the hardships of her career. Pauline tells her that not only has she lost the revenue from the Woodstock concert, but she will arrive in Fredericton too late for her second recital there and will have to pay the hall rental anyway. Christmas will be bleak this year.

Pauline toils on through the winter of 1900-1901 in the Maritimes, then begins touring Ontario. But it is a bitterly cold winter with heavy snows; attendances are down and many of her recitals have to be cancelled. By the first of April she has checked into The Graham House in Havelock, near Peterborough. She cannot leave because she has no money to pay her hotel bill. In desperation she writes to her old friend, Frank Yeigh, and begs for a loan. She describes her present circumstances as "a network of tragedy – too sad for human tongue to tell."

> Now could you without great inconvenience lend me…fifteen dollars to be repaid in a month's time? You could never quite imagine just "where I am at" or you would forgive me writing and asking this.
>
> Here I am, in Holy Week in Havelock – an economical town to pray in – also to eat in, and I *shall* be here all week.

She asks Yeigh not to tell her brother or her friend Harry O'Brien what she is asking of him. He already knows not to tell Eva. Pauline promises him that if he can spare the money, he will be doing more than churches or priests can do for her or himself "in the great Hereafter."

While she is waiting for Yeigh's response, Pauline receives an unexpected visitor. J. Walter McRaye has been giving elocution lessons in exchange for his board in nearby Peterborough when he learns that Pauline is only a tram ride away. This time he comes to see her hoping not only to become her partner but, convinced that he has acquired the necessary experience and ability, to also manage her tours. Pauline is impressed by his enthusiasm, but he is destined to be disappointed. She has just received word from Thomas Cornyn that he is willing to be her manager again and will partner her with his concert pianist wife, Clara. This arrangement promises to be very good for Pauline: she will only have to carry half the program, she will have the company of a woman on her long journeys, and their manager – eager to please his wife – will obviously take extra care when making accommodation and travel arrangements.

A few days later, Yeigh provides the money for Pauline to escape from The Graham House, and within a month she is sharing stages on the Ontario recital circuit with Clara Cornyn. The association is not a happy one. Their instant clash of personalities is made worse by the fact that Clara Cornyn expects to have top billing even though Pauline is the "name" performer. As well, two women on the same bill is not "good box office," and the program they provide is too "cultural" to attract customers in the smaller settlements.

Convinced that the poor houses are merely the result of playing Ontario in the heat of summer, Thomas Cornyn sends the two women to Newfoundland in late August. His timing seems to be right;

several British warships have just entered St. John's harbour. Pauline and Clara Cornyn's recital takes place in St. Patrick's Hall on August 27, with the Governor General, his wife, and the fleet admiral as their patrons. All the ships' officers and the town's elite attend, and the recital is a financial success.

Prepared to reap even greater benefits while the fleet is in, the two women schedule a second concert for Friday, August 30; the hall is almost empty. The next morning they send messengers throughout the city delivering dodgers announcing a special matinee for that afternoon; the matinee is also a disaster. In spite of two more weeks of travel by boat around the island to give recitals, they leave Newfoundland in mid-September poorer than when they arrived.

On October 9 a disenchanted Pauline wires Clifford Sifton for help. Will he please arrange train tickets to take herself and Clara Cornyn from Campbellton, New Brunswick, where they are stranded at present, to Montreal? She will repay him when she arrives in Ottawa in two weeks' time. Sifton, who has already pledged himself to help her if the need should arise, promptly buys the requested tickets – no questions asked.

In Ottawa, a weary Pauline bids goodbye to Clara Cornyn and cancels Thomas Cornyn's management contract. Next she writes a letter to J. Walter McRaye offering him a contract as her stage partner and manager. After four years of misfortunes with managers and partners, she is willing to take the risk. McRaye accepts by return mail.

McMaster University

The Cariboo stagecoach passes Lac La Hache, where Pauline and Walter perform in a hayshed and share the stage with B.C. Premier Richard McBride.

McMaster University

After her trip to the Cariboo, where she "slept like a baby, laughed like a child, and ate like a lumberjack," she writes an article for *Saturday Night*.

7

A New Partner

Offering J. Walter McRaye a contract is probably Pauline Johnson's most astute career decision. At forty years of age, she has no alternative to the recital circuit; she no longer expects someone to marry her and provide support while she indulges her passion for writing poetry. But to continue making her living as a recitalist, she must have a partner who will share her programs without fighting her for the spotlight and a manager who can be trusted to do the job without botching it or cheating her. McRaye is eager to do both on her terms.

Not that McRaye has suddenly become another Smily. Although he exudes confidence in his talents and has improved his act in the five years he has spent touring Canada and the United States – sometimes with fly-by-night stage companies, sometimes as a lone recitalist – McRaye will never have Smily's flair and professionalism nor his creative ability and improvisation skills. But unlike Smily, McRaye really wants to be Pauline's backup act, and he is eager to promote her shows and book halls and trains and hotels for her – first because she is the most popular recitalist in Canada and will therefore enhance his stage image, and second because she can provide him with a steady job.

McRaye is twenty-five years old when Pauline takes him on as her partner and manager. Possibly because of his nomadic existence, he is a markedly self-centred young man and ungenerous in his relations with other people. He is also not always truthful. Pauline's friends generally dislike him; Harry O'Brien sees him as an opportunist. Eva Johnson loathes him. Allen Johnson tolerates him until Pauline makes the mistake of taking McRaye along for a family canoeing vacation; after that Allen avoids him.

But the hardships of Pauline's ten years on the road have whittled away some of her rigid standards; she recognizes McRaye's shortcomings but knows instinctively that she has his complete loyalty. She also appreciates his sense of humour; though not a razor-edged wit like Smily, he is capable of entertaining her by lampooning the travelling patent-medicine men of the day and by inventing a whimsical zoo of invisible pets. As a result, instead of the distant business arrangement she established with Smily, she responds to McRaye's imperfections with motherliness.

McRaye makes his debut as Pauline's partner in Ottawa on November 6, 1901. The critics are not kind to Pauline on this occasion. "The numbers contributed by Miss Johnson," says the Ottawa *Citizen*, "had formed a part of her program on her last visit to Ottawa which detracted somewhat from their effect. They were given in her usual style, which is vigorous and energetic and, if rather exaggerated at times from an artistic standpoint, still bright and clever." The *Citizen*'s critic did like the Johnson-McRaye sketch "At the Ball" which takes place at "an insane asylum" where two visitors mistake each other for patients. "In this," says the reviewer, "Mr. McRaye got in his best work. His other numbers were slightly marred by an assumed harshness of voice and an upward drawl at the end of the lines. Barring these defects which will probably disappear as he gains experience, Mr. McRaye's renderings showed considerable talent, sympathy and insight. His acting as Captain Fielding in 'A Red Girl's Reasoning' was certainly very fine." Pauline is pleased that the performance has gone off this well; she knows she can help him overcome his voice problems.

The Ottawa recital is followed by a string of one-night stands in small-town Ontario. As they travel, Pauline conducts line rehearsals of the skits she has written for them, and each afternoon wherever possible they have full rehearsals in the halls where they will play that evening.

In spite of their success, Pauline is very tired when they arrive in Orillia in the third week of December. McRaye has booked the opera house here, and ticket sales have been brisk, but on the morning of the recital Pauline is ill. A doctor is called to the hotel immediately, but this time she has already made her own diagnosis. It is the disease that killed her father: erysipelas, a streptococcal infection with no known cure at this time. The first symptom Pauline notices is a raised reddish patch of skin next to her nose; as it expands across her face, blisters form on its surface. Chills and pain and fever set in. The doctor gives her morphine for the pain, and a nurse begins a bedside vigil. But Pauline's condition worsens as the infection invades her bloodstream and she develops "brain fever." Her temperature soars and she becomes delirious.

Christmas Day, 1901, passes without celebration as McRaye waits helplessly. Three days later Pauline's fever finally begins to subside, and on the last day of the year, he takes her to the home of Kate Washington, her cousin in Hamilton, to recuperate. But Pauline is almost unrecognizable. Erysipelas does not actually leave scars but the inflammatory reaction is slow to fade, and because of her prolonged high fever, all her hair has fallen out.

Yet on February 7, 1902, only six weeks after she became ill, Pauline and McRaye are on stage again in London, Ontario. They have no choice; they have run out of money. Although Pauline has never worn makeup, she copes with the disfigurement of her face by applying a thick coat of paint and powder over the inflammations. To camouflage her bald pate when she's onstage in her buckskin costume, she wears a wig, but it itches so much that when she is dressed in a ball gown, she wears a large picture hat, "just like a

Broadway chorus girl." She tells friends, "People say it is very becoming, and no one suspects the tragedy underneath."

Throughout February and March, McRaye sets a relaxed schedule of recitals while Pauline recovers her strength, but by May they are back to a steady pace of five or six performances a week. By this time they are in the Sudbury area, garnering great reviews, and heading west. On June 6 they check into the Leland Hotel in Winnipeg, although they have not booked a hall to perform in that city. Instead, Pauline invites all her old friends and members of the press up to her hotel suite and entertains them with stories of her adventures since she was last in the city in January 1900. She even makes jokes about her lost hair. And while it is unusual for Pauline to take time off in mid-tour for a mere social visit, there is a serious purpose in this one. She knows that in two short weeks the newspapers will be buzzing with the announcement of Charles Drayton's marriage to Lydia Howland, the only daughter of the president of the Imperial Bank of Canada. Pauline simply wants everyone in Winnipeg to see that she is perfectly happy without him.

McRaye makes plans to begin their summer tour of the Prairies in Regina. Pauline does her part by writing to Madame Henrietta Forget, the wife of the lieutenant-governor of the Northwest Territories, asking for the Forgets' patronage at their recital. "You may advertise your entertainment under our patronage," Madame Forget responds by return mail. "Moreover, we shall be pleased to have you at Government House during your stay in Regina. And if it is at all possible, we would like you to come for Coronation Day…" The coronation she is referring to is that of King Edward VII on June 26. McRaye, whose solo career never included invitations to the homes of such eminent people, is thrilled and promptly schedules their recital for the night after the Coronation festivities, assured that all Regina's elite will attend.

But on June 24, word comes from London that Edward must undergo an emergency appendectomy. This is a fairly new operation, and Pauline and McRaye – along with most of the King's other loyal subjects – attend prayer services instead of the planned celebrations. Two days later the King is declared out of danger, but a new date for the coronation can't be set until he is well enough to endure it. Pauline and McRaye can't wait that long, and they hold their recital on June 30. The Forgets and all their friends attend as promised, and the lieutenant-governor presents Pauline with an enormous bouquet of roses, which she carries on stage with her for her opening recitation.

They leave Regina on July 4, heading west on the CPR's Number One. Long after twilight they pull into Medicine Hat, only to be told that there is a washout ahead and that their train will have to wait in a siding overnight. The next morning the train goes a further 125 miles (201 km) west and stops at Gleichen in the heart of the Blackfoot Indian reserve. Pauline, writing a special report for Toronto's *Globe* newspaper, explains:

> We had come out of the east and its wheat lands of Manitoba, out of the drenching rains and unseasonable storms, into a per-

> fect July day, with the prairie swelling away to the north; westward, a horizon fringed with a glory of glistening white peaks where the royal old Rockies swept irregularly across the sky; southward, the lonely habitations of an erstwhile powerful tribe of Redmen.
>
> We had not halted very long when the Imperial Limited roared up abaft, and in another twelve hours a second Number One stood in to harbour. And then we learned the truth – two bridges down, one east, one west of Calgary. Number Two is stuck at Banff, the Imperial Limited, eastbound, tied up the gods alone know where. Never in the history of the CPR has traffic been so congested, never has the great Imperial Limited ceased its ninety-seven hour career across the continent.

For two days the CPR is host to more than six hundred people in the middle of the Indian reserve. Pauline has a marvellous holiday, meeting the motley assortment on board the three trains – everyone from an English lord and his new bride to a contingent of NWMP officers bound for the Yukon to American tourists to eastern European immigrants. The weather remains clear and hot, and the passengers keep themselves entertained collecting mushrooms, riding ponies rented from the Indians, and visiting a Blackfoot encampment.

On the third day the trains are moved to the edge of the Bow River, where the passengers discover that the bridge there has been completely shattered. A makeshift footbridge has been erected, and one by one they are helped across, railway employees trailing along behind with their luggage. Arriving in Calgary, they learn that "every hotel, Pullman car, boarding house, and even sample room was crowded, people boarded together under any and every roof possible..." Pauline and McRaye are now stuck here while the bridge to the west is reconstructed, but this is no tragedy for either of them. McRaye sets about hiring a hall and putting up posters, while Pauline calls on the mayor and CPR officials to be patrons for a gala recital. With so many people waiting in Calgary with nothing to do, the hall is packed that night, the next and the next.

The bridges rebuilt and the trains on schedule again, the two continue west for a prolonged tour of the Kootenay mining towns of Rossland, Fernie, Coal Creek, Sandon, Retallack, Nelson, Trout Lake, Greenwood, and Phoenix. The partners travel in style here because although this is rugged country, rail lines snake around mountains and along the lakeshores to connect the mines with their markets. Performance space is sometimes makeshift – at Camp McKinney the audience sits on benches hastily made from nail kegs and planks – but all the bigger settlements have opera houses or at least a church hall or two.

Pauline and McRaye draw full houses in these mining towns. The homesick miners, generally from England, Wales, or Northern Ireland, recognize the essential Britishness of Pauline's sentiments and her brand of humour. And since there are few ladies in these settlements, some of the men come just to look at Pauline in her lovely ball gown. Like royalty, she is also expected to tour their mines and give benefits for widows and maimed miners or to raise money to construct churches. But when they leave the Kootenays, the partners are considerably richer than when they arrived. Then it's on to the mining community of Fairview in the south Okanagan and north up the valley to Vernon at summer's end.

Although Pauline's hair is still unfashionably short and her face bears the outlines of the inflammations, her health is improving rapidly. And she is in her element in the west. For one thing, there is less competition here for audiences. In eastern Canada every large city is on the big American show circuits. Stock companies from New York bring elaborate productions like *Ben Hur* to Toronto, and the public flocks to see them. But in western Canada, only the towns along the border see real stage plays, and these are the smaller productions by companies based in San Francisco. Pauline has no trouble outdrawing them.

With nothing to worry her except writing and performing, she is beginning to glow again with her old vitality. And she is writing and publishing more than she has in years – poems, short stories, travel articles, opinion pieces. By the end of 1902 she is ready to publish a second book of her poems and she gathers together those which have been most popular as performance pieces. She subsidizes the venture with her share of the rental money from Chiefswood, her first from that source in three-and-a-half years. The book, called *Canadian Born* after her poem by that name, is released by the George Morang Publishing Company of Toronto in early 1903. It contains only thirty-one poems. The critics in general find it disappointing. "Poor book," Pauline writes to her friend O'Brien. "And half the poems it contains were accepted by *Harper's* and brought me some excellent notice. Well, I must try a novel now and get criticized for that."

But it isn't to novel-writing that Pauline turns her hand next. In the summer of 1903 on a camping and canoeing holiday in Ontario's Kawartha Lakes district, she begins her first experiments with adventure stories for boys, using her knowledge of native life, then adding yarns about the Mounties. But her best-selling work is still her adventure-travel stuff, and in late May 1904 she makes the most of a trip to Edmonton to add to her repertoire. The last patches of snow are still on the ground as Pauline and McRaye watch an exhausted dog train struggle into town, the sled runners grinding along on bare ground more often than on snow. Later that day she writes her poem "Train Dogs," then sets to work on the short story "The Haunting Thaw." After their Edmonton recital, the partners head for the Royal North-West Mounted Police (RNWMP) garrison at Fort Saskatchewan, where they are the guests of Inspector Charles Constantine and his wife. The inspector's stories also provide material for her later tales, and his wife, who is beloved by the men in the ranks, becomes the model for the heroine in her short story "Mother o' the Men."

The poem "Train Dogs" has a strange history. Pauline sends it first to *Outing* magazine but gets it back with a pencilled note in the margin suggesting that she could do better. In December 1904 it is published in *Rod and Gun*. They pay her seventy-five cents for the privilege; she sends it back to them, telling them that it is obvious they need it more than she does. Then, four years later, the poem suddenly appears on the cover of *Outing* credited to Owen E. McGillicuddy, and rumour has it that McGillicuddy has been paid twenty-five dollars for it. But it is all part of an elaborate hoax perpetrated by Pauline's good friend Bob Edwards, the publisher of the Calgary *Eye Opener*, who wants to prove that she had been discriminated against as a woman poet. At the same time, he is getting in a dig at his hated rival, Daniel McGillicuddy, the publisher of the Calgary *Daily News*, by implying that all McGillicuddys are cheats and frauds. It is actually Edwards who collects the twenty-five dollars for Pauline.

Back in British Columbia in the summer of 1904, Pauline and McRaye play the Kootenay mining towns again and travel north up the Okanagan Valley, ending at Kamloops in midsummer. The biggest adventure of all awaits them as they set off by horse and surrey into the hot, dry Cariboo country, heading for the mining town of Barkerville, the site of British Columbia's biggest gold strike thirty years earlier. There is only a small canopy on the surrey to protect them from the sun, but in spite of this being an 850-mile (1368-km) round trip, Pauline thrives on the rigours of the journey, and she is thrilled with the rustic log "mile-houses" where they stop each night. Afterwards Pauline tells friends that she "slept like a baby, laughed like a child, and ate like a lumberjack." Along the way the partners stage recitals, but there is no pressure to perform; this is a holiday, and their recitals only have to make enough to pay for the trip.

Wherever they stop, the pair are greeted with enthusiasm because performers seldom come this way. At Barkerville they step from their coach in front of Kelly's Hotel and promptly come under the proprietor's personal care. When he hears how much they are to be charged for a hall, he is incensed at such robbery and renegotiates the deal: four dollars for two nights. That evening they draw an audience of 210 miners, and since seats are going at the staggering price of $2.50 each, the partners do well here. To show his gratitude for their fine treatment, McRaye invites all the men in the audience into Kelly's to drink the proprietor's health. The bill comes to sixty-seven dollars.

On their way south again, they stop at Lac la Hache. There's no hall here, but a farmer offers the use of a large cedar shake hayshed near the lake and sends riders out to announce that there will be a show that night. Just as the recital is about to begin, there is a commotion outside, and two men in city clothes stand in the doorway. They are British Columbia's premier, Richard McBride – otherwise known as "Glad Hand Dick," and his adviser, Charlie Wilson, touring the Cariboo in a by-election campaign. Pauline agrees to share her stage; she and McRaye will perform from eight till ten, the premier will give a campaign speech from ten to midnight, and then they will all dance till dawn. And that is what they do.

It is a most successful "holiday" trip in other ways too. Pauline writes the story of this adventure for *Toronto Saturday Night*, and over the next year it is reprinted in dozens of journals right across the country.

Later she revises it as "Coaching on the Cariboo Trail" for *Canadian Magazine*.

Pauline and McRaye complete their tour of British Columbia at the end of August 1904 and head for the Prairies. They begin 1905 in Ontario, carry on to New York State, then go north into New Brunswick. July and August are reserved for a tour of Ontario, then it's back to the newly created provinces of Alberta and Saskatchewan for the early fall, ending the year in Manitoba.

Since her mother's death, Pauline seldom goes home to Brantford for Christmas, and in 1905 she and McRaye celebrate the season in the lumbering town of Rainy River, close to the American border. Almost the entire settlement joins them for Christmas dinner in the little hotel where they are staying, and the proprietor lays out a spread of deer, bear, beaver, partridge, grouse, and chicken as well as the customary turkey. Afterwards, Pauline entertains the children with Indian tales while the adults play parlour games, then a fiddler spins reels and two-steps while they all dance.

In this festive atmosphere Pauline announces that she and McRaye have booked passage to England for April 1906.

McMaster University

Vancouver's Chief Joe Capilano, spokesman for a delegation to see King Edward VII, meets Pauline in London and they become lifelong friends. Left to right: Interpreter Simon Pierre, Chief Charlie Filpaynem, Chief Joe Capilano, and Chief Basil.

8

London and the Literary Life

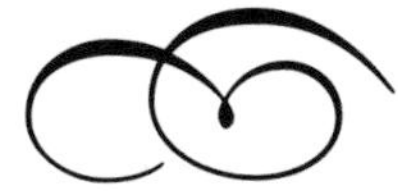

Pauline and McRaye perform in Ontario in the early months of 1906 while they prepare for London. Ever since her success there in 1894, she has been determined to return; the main obstacle has been how to finance the venture. She came very close to her goal in 1900 when she borrowed money against the Chiefswood rental to go to Australia and then England, but her plans were dashed when Wurz stole her money. With McRaye as manager, however, her financial worries appear to be over. The two of them have had four years of consistently good box office; in fact, in Peterborough in early February 1906 they play to the largest audience that has ever turned out for a performance in the history of the town.

The main factor in her renewed popularity with the public has been her improved health. Since her devastating attack of erysipelas in December 1901, Pauline has suffered no major illnesses; she has, in fact, grown quite plump and matronly looking. And with McRaye taking care of the business end of touring, she has been able to conserve her energies for writing and performing. As a result, she has revitalized their recitals, both by adding new material to their programs and by performing with her old vigour and confidence.

However, Pauline still has extravagant tastes, and even the increased box-office take has not been enough to maintain both herself and McRaye on a daily basis as well as finance a season in London. But she has made up her mind that this time she will go, and on August 2, 1905, she takes a drastic step. She writes to her old friend Ernest Thompson Seton, who now lives in the United States, where his animal stories have made him famous. Can he find a buyer for her wampum belt?

> [It] is one of the League wampum belts used at the time of the confederation of the Five Nations, now the Six Nations.... I came by this belt most fortunately as, when the old fire-keeper died, his son took upon himself to dispose of the fifty-seven ancient national belts, thus destroying our archives. My belt is one of the largest and most famous. It was the identical one my grandfather selected to hold in his hands when the Six Nations representative chiefs were photographed for the late Dr. Hale's book and translation of the

> Iroquois rites.... I am compelled to part with this belt if I would get to England again. It is my only very valuable asset and you may be well assured that my reasons are few when I even think of parting with it, for wampum is the most precious of all Indian relics, and this particular belt is of most historical value and cannot possibly be duplicated.
>
> The wampum is valued at $1600 as all Hiawatha League belts are of about such value. But of course I would accept much less for it....

With Seton's help, negotiations with an American buyer are completed successfully, and McRaye books passage for himself and Pauline on Canadian Pacific's *Lake Champlain*, leaving New York for Southampton on April 19, 1906.

The partners cross the border to perform in Johnstown, New York, in early April, then entrain for New York City where they visit Eva Johnson, who is now working there. Pauline does not tell Eva about the sale of the wampum belt, but Eva has something else to complain about. She is appalled that Pauline is planning to take McRaye with her to London.

"What will people think?" she storms. "He has no culture whatsoever!"

"He is my partner, Eva," Pauline responds.

"I grant you he is a fair entertainer and very bright and jolly, but he has no refinement!"

Pauline needs McRaye as much as he needs her. Without him she would be doomed to more incompetent and dishonest managers and burdened with giving entire performances alone. And she would have no time to write. But Eva cannot appreciate this, and the bitterness between the two women continues.

After an uneventful Atlantic crossing, Pauline settles into an elegant third floor apartment at 53 St. James Square, sublet from friends and complete with staff. She chooses the front sitting room and adjoining bedroom for her use because they look out on the beautiful Church of St. James Norland; prepared for a long stay, she hangs deerskins and her tomahawks on the walls along with other mementoes of her father's people.

London's social life has changed since the pleasure-loving King Edward came to the throne. Hostesses no longer entertain their guests with drawing-room performances; now they hold bridge whist parties, go dancing after dinner, or make up theatre parties. As a result, there is a much smaller market for the partners' talents in the homes of the wealthy and titled than there was when Pauline was here in 1894. But knowing times have changed, they have registered ahead with the Keith Rowse Entertainment Agency, and they have been advertised in the London papers as "garden party entertainers," fresh from America. To become known to the general public as well, the two also rent London's posh Steinway Hall for a performance on July 16.

Then once again Pauline sets out to find patrons, but this time she has targeted prominent Canadians: Lord and Lady Strathcona. As Donald A. Smith, he came from Scotland as a Hudson's Bay Company apprentice and rose through the ranks to become governor of the company. Most famous for his role in building Canada's railways, he also had a hand in this country's politics and finances and was rewarded with the job of Canada's high commissioner in London and a knighthood in 1897. His London home is in Grosvenor Square while his country home is the beautiful Knebworth estate in Hertfordshire. He is eighty-six when Pauline comes to ask him to be her patron, but age has not dimmed his interest in beautiful and talented ladies. Of course, he and Lady Strathcona will be Pauline's patrons.

Another Canadian to whom Pauline carries a letter of introduction is Sir Gilbert Parker, who had left Canada for Australia as a very young man to make his reputation as a journalist. Arriving in London in 1890, he launched a career as a novelist and by 1902 had won himself fame and a knighthood. He and his wife are delighted to become involved in promoting Pauline's Steinway Hall concert. Parker is on good terms with most of London's newspaper and magazine editors, and he undertakes to send them Pauline's publicity material and invite all their critics to review the show.

It is Parker's intervention that brings an immediate request for an interview from the prestigious literary journal, *M.A.P.* Pauline, who is always "onstage" for reviewers, treats this one to stories of the more humorous events from her travels.

> Miss Johnson tells a good yarn of a certain little town in Newfoundland. Arriving on the day of the performance, she was annoyed

> to find that the walls were very poorly billed [few posters were displayed]. The local bill-poster was summoned and questioned. He indignantly protested that he had done his best and took Miss Johnson to the end of the main street. There he posted up a couple of bills and asked her to retreat for a little distance and after a while a herd of goats appeared on the scene and made straight for the posters, stripping them off the walls to lick the paste underneath.
>
> "Guess them goats want to digest your show," the bill-poster said.

When the reporter shows an interest in her buckskin costume, Pauline regales her with the story of the lady's maid who had helped her dress for a performance a few days earlier. To avoid confusion, Pauline explained what each part of the costume was for, ending with, "And these long, beaded things are my leggings."

"Oh, I quite understand, ma'am," responded the young woman. "I've heard that Canadian ladies wear toboggans on their feet."

A highlight of the early summer for Pauline and McRaye is the Strathconas' July 14 garden party at Knebworth Hall, attended by 1,500 people, including every Canadian of any social standing living in England. Special trains leave King's Cross all afternoon to accommodate the guests. They are entertained by two bands, and an army of white-gloved waiters deliver tea, sandwiches, and cakes to tables set up under striped marquees on the lawns. Pauline meets many old friends: the Marchioness of Donegal and the Duchess of Montrose, for whom she had entertained guests in 1894; Sir Charles Tupper, who tells everyone how he introduced Pauline to society on her last visit; the Countess of Worford; the Duke of Argyll, who had come as Canada's Governor General to visit the Johnsons at Chiefswood when Pauline was young; and "whole-souled and Irish" Lady Helen Blake, who in 1894 had "spoiled her dreadfully." And they all promise to attend the upcoming recital.

Two evenings later, Steinway Hall is crowded, and the applause for the partners is prolonged and enthusiastic. What they present is virtually the same program that Canadians have been seeing from them for years, but it is new to London and that is what matters. Afterwards, Pauline's dressing room is crowded with well-wishers, among them Theodore Watts-Dunton, who had given *The White Wampum* such a favourable review in 1895. But he has not met the author before, and when he introduces himself, Pauline calls for silence. She then announces that it was to his review that she owed most of her literary success. There are tears in her eyes as she thanks him, pressing his hand.

"You must dine with us at The Pines," Watts-Dunton responds. "Algernon must meet you!"

The Algernon he refers to is the poet Algernon Swinburne, whom Watts-Dunton rescued from a life of alcoholism thirty years earlier. When they meet a few days later at The Pines, Pauline sees a tiny man with a wispy moustache and goatee, bald except for a fringe of rusty hair. They talk of poets and poetry, and Pauline confesses how much of her own work was inspired by his. She leaves a lasting impression on Swinburne, and several years later he tells Canada's Charles G.D. Roberts, "I could never forget Pauline!"

Thanks to the efforts of Gilbert Parker, the press had come out in force for the Steinway recital, and reviews appear in more than a dozen newspapers and journals; all are favourable. And though the partners have entertained regularly at soirées and garden parties since early June, they are now in such demand that they cannot accept all the engagements.

But Parker and his wife are responsible for an even more important event in Pauline's London visit. At one of their soirées, Pauline is approached by a middle-aged gentleman.

"You are Miss Johnson, the Indian poetess, I believe. My friend Parker tells me you might be available to write a little something for my newspaper."

"And you are...?"

"Pearson. I have some papers in the city."

But Sir Arthur Pearson has more than "some papers." He actually owns thirty newspapers, the most important one being the *Daily Express* of London.

"Certainly, Mr. Pearson," Pauline responds as she recognizes his name. "I would be pleased to write for your paper."

"Good. My editor, Mr. Fraser, will call on you."

Pauline is elated. One of her main goals in coming to London again is to find more markets for her writing, primarily her articles and stories. She already contributes regularly to Canadian and American magazines, but being published in England will add to the prestige of her work and make it more in demand at home. Besides, writers are paid better in England; she has ample proof of that in the success of her new friend, Gilbert Parker.

Two days later Malcolm Fraser invites Pauline to his office to discuss the type of article she will write for the *Daily Express*. They agree on three full-page articles on Mohawk life. "The Lodge of the Law-Makers" is the first to appear, then "The Silent News-Carrier," and finally, the most famous one, "A Pagan in St. Paul's," published on August 3, 1906. It is Pauline's attempt to see London through the eyes of someone from her grandfather's generation, coming to see the "camp" of the Great White Father, King Edward, "the ruler of many lands, lodges and tribes, in the hollow of whose hands is the peace that rests between the once hostile Red Man and White." As Pauline's hero stands outside the King's "council-house" by the River Thames, he hears a choir singing in nearby St. Paul's Cathedral and goes to investigate. Amid the worshippers, he listens as "the music beats in my ears like a storm hurling through the fir forest, like the distant rising of an Indian war-song; it sweeps up those mighty archways until the gray dome above me fades, and in its place the stars come out to look down, not on these palefaces kneeling to worship, but on a band of my own people in my own land, who also do honour to the Manitou of all nations." He hears "the beat of the Indian drum and the turtle rattle that set time for the dancers' feet" as they conduct rites of worship by sacrificing a white dog in the campfires' glow. The ceremony over, the drum beats fade, and he becomes aware once more of the choir voices of St. Paul's. And it comes to him that though the forms of worship may differ, White Man and Red Man worship the same Great Spirit, desiring only that He "will forever smoke His pipe of peace, for peace is between Him and His children for all time."

Three days after "A Pagan in St. Paul's" appears in the *Daily Express*, three real native Canadians arrive in London. From British Columbia, they are Chief Joe Capilano of the Squamish band, Chief Charlie Filpaynem of the Cowichans, and Chief Basil of the Bonapartes, and they have come to place their grievances before the King. Their lands have been encroached on by settlers, fishermen, miners, loggers, and railroad men, and they have borne it all in silence. But now new game laws deny native people the right to hunt deer in spring and summer, and new restrictions have been placed on freshwater fishing. No one in Victoria will listen to them because none of British Columbia's native tribes have signed treaties with either the provincial or federal governments. Their last resort is an appeal to the King himself.

When the three arrive at London's Euston station after their long journey, they are rescued from the throng of reporters by a young man from Lord Strathcona's office. He finds them accommodation, then sends word to Britain's secretary for the colonies that the next move is his. Through their interpreter, the secretary attempts to persuade them to go home, but the chiefs are adamant: they are not leaving until they speak with the King. After much consultation in high places, it is decided that since the press has taken such an interest in the three men, denying them a royal audience would provoke very unfavourable public reaction. Unfortunately, the King is out of the city all week at Cowes for the annual regatta, so an audience with him will have to be delayed until his return. The problem is what to do with the chiefs in the meantime?

And then Lord Strathcona has an idea. "My dear Miss Johnson, will you speak to them? We've been unable to make them understand why they must wait."

Pauline and McRaye have been enjoying a brief holiday in Berkshire, but she takes the train to London and goes immediately to call on the three chiefs. Not that Pauline speaks the language of any of the chiefs. What she has to offer is a small knowledge of Chinook jargon, the hybrid language developed for trading purposes on the west coast. Originally a mixture of the Chinook tongue from the tribe by that name on the Columbia River, plus English and French, it became even more hybrid when words from other tribal languages were added as needed. It is fully sufficient for the purpose intended – though not for carrying on long conversations.

The reporters scurrying after Pauline only hear her greet the chiefs with, "Klahowya Tillicum skookum," before the door closes behind her. The conversation that follows is not recorded, but it is most probable that it is carried on primarily between Pauline and Chief Joe Capilano as he generally acts as spokesman for the group. And although she can do nothing to speed their audience with the King, when she leaves, they know at least that they have one person on their side in this vast city. And Pauline has begun a friendship with Chief Joe that she will cherish in the years ahead.

The next day the reporters, who assume that all North American Indians speak the same language, besiege Pauline. They want her to act as interpreter while they interview the chiefs. Pauline declines.

The King and Queen receive the chiefs in the throne room on August 13. When they have trudged halfway up the long room, the King steps down from the platform and comes to greet them, shaking Chief Joe's hand, then leading the three men to the Queen. Years later, Chief Joe tells Pauline, "Now you see what great men do. Little man he stay on platform and make we chiefs walk up to him, but the Great White Chief he big man, the biggest man in the world...." After a twenty-minute discussion of their problems, the three have the assurances of the King that he will see that "the matter is made right," although it might take some time.

Before the chiefs depart from London the next day, Pauline visits with them once more to wish them Godspeed. On August 15 they head home as steerage passengers on the Canadian Pacific's *Lake Manitoba*; each of them carries a gold medallion featuring likenesses of the King and Queen, given to them by the King himself.

In early September Pauline and McRaye return to the recital circuit, their popularity increased by the publication of "A Pagan in St. Paul's" and Pauline's part in the chiefs' visit. Although these two events bring broader recognition for both her writing and her performances in England, they also cause Pauline bouts of homesickness for Canada. In October at a performance of Somerset Maugham's play *The Land of Promise* at the Haymarket Theatre, McRaye looks over to find her paying no attention to the scene onstage, a mock-up of a homesteader's cabin.

"Not a bit like the real thing, is it?" he whispers.

Pauline smiles and shakes her head.

Then after a minute, McRaye asks, "How would you like to be back on the old Cariboo Trail right now?"

Pauline nods assent. She certainly would. At intermission, she begins writing on the back of her program, and before the curtain rises for the third act, she shows McRaye the first draft of her new poem, "The Trail to Lillooet."

By mid-November the partners are booked to return home. Financially, it has been a highly successful season for them, and through the efforts of both old and new contacts, the prospects for the coming one are equally good. Pauline's friend, Lady Helen Blake, just returned from five years as the Governor General's lady in Jamaica, has set the wheels in motion for Pauline and McRaye to tour the British West Indies early in the new year to take advantage of the annual tourist influx there. She even arranges for the new Governor General, Sir Alexander Swettenham, to be their patron. George Alexander, actor and producer, has introduced them to the agent for the American Slayton Lyceum Society, resulting in the partners being hired for a circuit of the midwestern states in the summer of 1907. And Sir Arthur Pearson will be pleased to take more of Pauline's writing for the *Daily Express*.

For McRaye there is a bonus. He has wooed and won the hand of Lucy Webling, the youngest member of a family of recitalists. Pauline has known them since 1890 when two of the Webling sisters – Peggy and Josephine – lived in Brantford; five years later three of them – Peggy, Rosalind, and Lucy – began touring Canada, returning to London in 1898. Rosalind Webling then took ship back to Canada to marry photographer George Edwards of Vancouver, and each time Pauline and McRaye have come to Vancouver they have visited with the Edwards. Now at last McRaye has met Lucy and fallen in love. A gifted young actress and dancer, she has been on the stage for nineteen of her twenty-six years, and when she meets McRaye she is playing the part of "Mimi" in William Haviland's production of *The Only Way*. Since the play is a hit, the cast have settled in for a long run, so that when Pauline and McRaye leave for Canada in late November, Lucy must remain behind to complete her contract. But she and McRaye are pledged to marry in a few years' time.

On her second trip to England, in 1906, Pauline performs with McRaye in both public recitals and private salons and develops new markets for her writing.

The Canadian Indian Poet-Entertainer
E. PAULINE JOHNSON
(TEKAHIONWAKE)

IN READINGS FROM HER OWN BOOK
"THE WHITE WAMPUM"
LEGENDS, POEMS AND STORIES

NOW TOURING ENGLAND

McMaster University

Still staunchly pro-British, Pauline is furious when the Chautauqua bills her as an American Indian during her tour of small town America in 1907.

McMaster University

9

Chautauqua

Pauline and McRaye celebrate Christmas 1906 in Montreal, then head for Halifax in early January to embark for Jamaica. But they never make their planned tour of the British West Indies. On January 14, 1907, an earthquake levels the city of Kingston, Jamaica, with the loss of over a thousand lives. Since Kingston was to have been their primary destination, they abort the trip and settle for a wintry tour of the Maritimes.

By the beginning of March they are back in Ontario, but here the partners leave the recital circuit for separate four-month holidays. This much time off is an unusual luxury for them, but they have earned it with the financial success of their London venture, and they will need it to get ready for the grind of a season in the midwestern states on the chautauqua circuit. McRaye takes his holiday with his mother in Brockville. Pauline begins hers in Hamilton as a guest of her cousin Kate Washington. For nearly five years Kate's home has served as Pauline's official address, and Kate has been forwarding Pauline's mail to hotels and post offices along the recital circuit. This time when Pauline arrives, the mail awaiting her includes requests from several magazine editors for more stories. During the next month Pauline writes steadily, preparing Mountie and Indian adventures for several boys' magazines and stories about Indian women for *Mother's Magazine*.

After a month in her cousin's home, Pauline takes the train to Brantford to meet her brother Allen. They check into the Kerby House to share a quiet week together, and Pauline gets to know Allen's fiancée. At forty-nine, he is to marry Floretta Katherine Maracle, a Mohawk schoolteacher. He will be the only one of the Johnson children to escape his elder brother's prediction that they will all be "waifs and strays" because they never learned how to love.

On April 27 Pauline returns to England aboard the *Lake Erie* and for the next six weeks enjoys the sights of London without having to worry about performing. She is, however, looking for more markets for her stories and so keeps in touch with people like Sir Arthur Pearson and Sir Gilbert Parker. She is also searching for something else: a place to settle and write after she leaves the recital platform. London seems an obvious choice since she has already acquired a reputation here, and many other Canadians – including Parker – have successfully made the transition from colony to mother country, gaining wealth and even knighthoods in the process. But her investigations tell her that her standard of living would be difficult to maintain in Britain, especially if her rugged Redcoat and fearless Indian stories didn't gain wide readership. And she must face the distinct possibility that the Mohawk Princess might be simply a one-season wonder in this great and fickle metropolis. When she heads for home in mid-June to attend her brother's wedding, she has given up on the idea of retiring in London. The return trip takes her from Southampton via Cherbourg on the U.S. Mail steamer *St. Paul* to arrive in New York on June 19.

Allen's wedding and their holidays over, the partners rendezvous in Toronto to prepare the program for their new tour. The American Slayton Lyceum Society to whom they are contracted is an agent for chautauquas and lyceums all over the United States. Both events are forms of outdoor summer school. The first lyceum – named after the place where the philosopher Aristotle taught long ago in Greece – was a week-long educational event for adults held in Massachusetts in the summer of 1826. The concept was instantly popular, and organizers all over the United States began inviting debaters and lecturers to their towns for a week each summer to discuss and educate. The first chautauqua – started in a town by that name in upstate New York – was the religious equivalent of the lyceum, organized to educate Sunday school teachers and church workers. By the time Pauline and McRaye are hired by the Slayton Society to perform in 1907, the two institutions have merged, with both serving up evangelical religion and education in equal portions. And since half the small towns in America now feature one of these summer events, agencies like the Slayton Lyceum Society have taken on the job of setting up circuits and coordinating the tours of the performers.

A small number of the communities hosting these events have built bandshells to improve acoustics, but most towns hold their events outdoors or in the shelter of a large tent set up in a field. In the midwest much of the audience is drawn from the surrounding countryside, farmers happy to take a break from chores halfway between seeding time and harvest. Whole families arrive by horse and buggy to set up their own sleeping tents around the main tent; some cook their meals over campfires, others buy their meals from kitchens set up around the perimeter of the grounds. While most of the townfolk in the audience have basic schooling, the average farmer has been too busy wresting a living from the soil to consider education for himself or his children, and, in any case, he is doubtful of its value to farm life. To him the real worth of the chautauqua is its religious content and the once-a-year opportunity to get together with his neighbours.

Pauline and McRaye begin their chautauqua ordeal directly after the fourth of July holiday. The timing is fortunate because Pauline's health remains good and she is well-rested. On the chautauqua/lyceum circuit, performers have to be hardy. They are hired for ten weeks of performance and are so tightly scheduled that they must travel steadily from town to town, delivering one or sometimes two performances before catching the train to the next performance stop. They sleep on trains, catnap on park benches, and eat bean suppers in camp kitchens. The show goes on whether it pours rain or blows a tornado; many of the campgrounds in the wet summer of 1907 are ankle-deep in soupy mud.

Their first performances are in Indiana farm country where McRaye is listed on the programs as a French-Canadian *habitant* with Pauline as an American Indian. McRaye has problems with his billing, but Pauline is incensed with hers. She still holds a grudge against the Americans for their expulsion of the Mohawk people from their traditional lands in upstate New York after the War of Independence. Staunchly pro-British – as her father and grandfather were before her – she regards anything American as somewhat inferior.

In spite of these sentiments, she has always enjoyed performing in the eastern United States, especially when sponsored by the Indian Association. However, this has had more to do with the sophistication of her audiences than their nationality. Her adventures in the plains states have been far less happy, due mainly to the prevailing midwestern attitude toward Indians. In this part of the country the so-called "Indian Wars" raged on well after the middle of the century; it was here that U.S. General Philip Sheridan, setting out in 1867 on one of the last major campaigns against Indian tribes, uttered his famous line, "The only good Indians I ever saw were dead." This statement still reflects the general feelings of midwesterners, and when Pauline arrives to play this area, the locals regard a recital by an Indian as something of a freak show, a chance to show their children what a real live Indian looks like.

Pauline's reaction to this treatment is to become haughty and more distant, but she does not soft-pedal her native heritage. The program she delivers is weighted heavily with her Indian poems, especially ones such as "A Cry from an Indian Wife" and "The Cattle Thief" which make her audiences squirm guiltily. Dressed in her buckskins, she becomes the daughter of the Cattle Thief, protecting his dead body from desecration;

You have killed him, but you shall not dare to touch him now he's dead.
You have cursed and called him a Cattle Thief, though you robbed him first of bread –
Robbed him and robbed my people – look there, at that shrunken face,
Starved with a hollow hunger we owe to you and to your race.
What have you brought but evil and curses since you came?
How have you paid us for our game? How paid us for our land?
By a *book*, to save our souls from the sins *you* brought in your other hand.
Go back with your new religion, we never have understood
Your robbing an Indian's *body* and mocking his *soul* with food.

Go back with your new religion, and find – if find you can –
The *honest* man you have ever made from out a *starving* man.
You say your cattle are not ours, your meat is not our meat;
When *you* pay for the land you live in, *we'll* pay for the meat we eat.
Give back our land and our country, give back our herds of game;
Give back the furs and the forests that were ours before you came;
Give back the peace and the plenty. Then come with your new belief,
And blame, if you dare, the hunger that drove him to be a thief.

Her audiences are left gasping. But rather than change their attitudes toward native people, the farmers only marvel that an Indian can write real poems and behave with company manners just like a white person. The reviews of her performances, however, are excellent.

There are few women on the circuit of chautauquas that Pauline and McRaye are following. A small wren-like woman named Elma B. Smith gives a two-and-a-half-hour concert of "child impersonations and bird warblings," and the Cleveland Ladies Philharmonic "surpasses all expectations" with their concert, expecially their cornet and trombone solos. But most of the performers are men: politicians, preachers, professional orators and recitalists, homespun philosophers, novelists and poets. Their lecture topics are established with the lyceum office when they sign on for the circuit to make sure there will be no surprises for local organizers. Each speaker repeats the same rigidly memorized speech in every town – some carrying on for as much as three hours – never varying their hand gestures and emphasizing the same words each time by pounding on the lectern. They are, however, expected to make it sound spontaneous every time. All the speeches are sincere and uplifting; they are seldom humorous.

After Indiana, the partners travel west to Iowa, then Nebraska, south into Colorado and Kansas, then east again in late August into Missouri. As their travel arrangements seldom coincide with those of other performers or lecturers, they rarely share more than a brief conversation about the weather while waiting to go onstage. But on the Missouri leg of their circuit they ride the Wabash Railroad in the company of William Jennings Bryan, the famous lawyer and perennial presidential candidate for the Republican party, who is scheduled to perform on the same program as they are in the town of St. Joseph. They are delayed when a train wreck occurs farther along the line, and it is four o'clock in the morning when they finally arrive. All the hotels are full because there's an Elks convention in town, so the three of them find a park bench. Here McRaye snoozes while Pauline and Bryan discuss politics until a restaurant opens for breakfast. Bryan is philosophical about the train wreck; in his two campaigns to become U.S. president this is the third time the Wabash line has delayed him with a washout. Later in the day when the St. Joseph's newspaper comes out, there's a cartoon of Bryan on the front page. It shows him sitting in the midst of a smash-up with the Wabash line on one side of him and another rail line marked "White House" on the other. The caption has Bryan shaking his head and saying, "Three times on this line and twice on this!" McRaye asks him to autograph his copy of the newspaper and Bryan complies good-naturedly, writing on it, "Not hurt yet. William J. Bryan." McRaye doesn't let on that part of his onstage stock-in-trade for many years was a parody of Bryan.

In Illinois in early September it is raining so hard that roads and bridges are washed out, trains are delayed, and they are repeatedly late for performance dates. Most of the chautauqua grounds are flooded, tents have collapsed into the mud, but they are still required to fulfil their contracts. They perform under umbrellas and hastily improvised awnings.

The partners complete their contract with the Slayton Lyceum Society in Illinois in the second week of September. By the 15th they are playing Boston sponsored by the Massachusetts Indian Association. The audience is refined and literate, and Pauline, once more in her element, puts on a stunning performance. At the reception afterwards she is beseiged by members of the city's literary set, all competing for the honour of entertaining her at dinners and soirées.

A few days later, she gives an interview to an admiring *Boston Herald* reporter who is dazzled by her wit and brilliant conversation. She is propounding her views on the American attitude to native people and the treatment she received in the midwest when the reporter suggests by his glance that he is skeptical of her theories.

"Ah, I understand that look!" she tells him. "You're going to say I'm not like other Indians, that I'm not representative. That's not strange. Cultivate an Indian, let him show his aptness and you Americans say he is an exception. Let a bad quality crop out and you stamp him as an Indian immediately." She is smiling her white-toothed smile all the time she is speaking but there is no mistaking the anger behind her words.

On October 5, 1907, Pauline and McRaye stop briefly in Winnipeg to organize a fresh tour. It is two years since they played western Canada and it is country ripe for the picking. Billing themselves as direct from London and from the American chautauqua circuit, they work their way northwest towards Prince Albert and Saskatoon, performing in every hamlet along the way. Their welcome is overwhelming. In Edmonton Pauline has a brief reunion with her old friend Ernest Thompson Seton, who is returning from an arctic safari, then the partners head for British Columbia's Okanagan and Kootenay valleys. By the beginning of December they are back on the Prairies for a winter tour. April sees them in New Brunswick, and by the middle of June they have played their way across Nova Scotia and Prince Edward Island.

Once again it is time for a holiday break. McRaye chooses Ontario for his time off, but Pauline entrains for Vancouver. After checking into the Hotel Vancouver on June 29, she sends a message to Chief Joe Capilano. May she visit him? He responds by sending his son Mathias in a canoe, and the two paddle to the Capilano band's reserve on the North Shore together. Pauline is welcomed warmly by Chief Joe and his wife and spends the afternoon in earnest conversation with them. When she leaves, she is given the use of a light canoe for the duration of her stay in Vancouver.

For the next six weeks – a rainless, cloudless July and August – when Pauline isn't in her hotel room writing stories, she is paddling the little canoe along the city's shorelines. Her favourite place is the upper reach of Burrard Inlet's Coal Harbour, which she renames Lost Lagoon because it is inaccessible at low tide. Years later, when the construction of a causeway turns this end of the harbour into a permanent lagoon, the city fathers rechristen it with the name she has given it.

Pauline is mainly on a scouting mission in Vancouver. On the day of her arrival in the city, she tells the Vancouver *World*'s reporter that she has come for a month, then adds mysteriously, "Maybe longer. There is no place in Canada that has a warmer spot in my heart than Vancouver." Is this little city a suitable place to retire? It is four years since she has last seen it, and it has changed. The population, now almost 100,000 strong, has acquired a veneer of sophistication, with literary societies, three well-attended theatres, and three newspapers that would provide markets for her writing. At the same time, the cost of living here is far lower than it is in the cities of eastern Canada or in London.

On July 7 the contralto Eileen Maguire gives a concert at the Hotel Vancouver. At a reception afterwards, Pauline is introduced to her and an immediate bond is formed between the two women. If she should happen to settle in the city, Pauline inquires, would Maguire consider sharing the platform with her for an occasional concert? The singer is delighted to accept as long as the concerts would not take her far from the city as she has her family's needs to consider.

By the time Pauline leaves Vancouver on August 14, she has made up her mind to retire to a writing life in Vancouver. The only thing left to decide is when.

McCrae collection

Some people say J. Walter McRaye is self-centred, but Pauline thinks he is a good manager and a stage partner who won't fight her for the spotlight.

10

The Final Tour

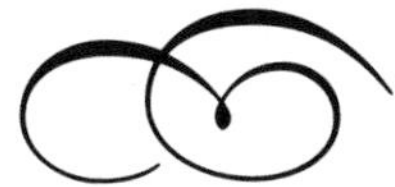

J. Walter McRaye knows that the recital circuit no longer holds any allure for Pauline, but he hopes to delay the day when she will abandon him. Although Lucy Webling will become his new stage partner after their marriage, she is still under contract to perform in England for another year. Can Pauline wait that long? And can McRaye hope to draw an audience when Pauline is not on the program?

Pauline has been touring for sixteen years and she is tired of being homeless, but for McRaye's sake, she agrees to continue for one more year. In September 1908 they launch their final circuit together. They play Ontario, then cross the border to perform in Cleveland and Pittsburg. Pauline spends Christmas with her cousin in Hamilton, then the partners set off across the Prairies for three and a half months of one-night stands.

She does not announce this as a farewell tour, but she does confide in close friends along the way that this is the last time she will be coming to entertain them. There are tears, of course, but not from Pauline, who always guards her emotions from public view. And sad as they are to be losing her, her friends are convinced that retirement is overdue; Pauline looks tired. There are dark shadows under her eyes and she is losing weight.

On May 6 in Vancouver's Pender Auditorium, Pauline announces her intention to settle in Vancouver for good. Her audience is ecstatic. But the final tour is not over yet; while waiting for Lucy to arrive, the partners work their way from town to town up the Fraser Valley, through the Okanagan and up the Nicola Valley. They make their last public appearance together in Kamloops on August 23, 1909.

The next day, McRaye and Lucy Webling are married in Christ Church Cathedral, Vancouver's most fashionable church. The bride, given in marriage by her brother-in-law George Edwards, is exquisite in a gown of Mechlin lace brought from London. Telegrams of congratulations arrive from Lucy's friends, some of the greatest names on the London stage: Ellen Terry, Lewis Waller, and Sir George Alexander. After a three-day honeymoon in Victoria, the couple set out in the company of singer Eileen Maguire on the first McRaye Company tour. All the portents are for a happily-ever-after marriage and stage partnership – although within six years the McRayes will part company.

At forty-seven, Pauline is officially retired and now she must find a permanent home. Fortunately, in early September an apartment becomes vacant in an almost new building at 1117 Howe Street in the city's West End, just a few blocks from the shops in one direction and from Stanley Park in the opposite one. Jubilantly, she sends off messages to Allen and her cousin Kate to ship the trunks and crates she has left in storage with them. Most of her belongings have been packed away since her mother died eleven years earlier, and she has entirely forgotten what is in some of the cases. The apartment is not large – two small bedrooms, a sitting room, kitchen, and bathroom – but there is room in the sitting room for the round Mission oak table and chair that had come from Chiefswood, a couch, and several chairs. She decorates the rooms with the mementoes collected on her travels and the china, crystal, and silverware that was her mother's.

When it is all in place, she begins writing in earnest. For the first time since she began touring in 1892, she can sit at her own desk in her own room to write and even leave it spread out when she retires for the day. There are no trains to catch, no costumes to repair, no audience to please. But this lack of stress makes it hard at first to write, and it isn't until she establishes a routine of writing, walking, and entertaining friends that the work begins to flow from her pen once more.

For the last five years she has written the stories promised to *Mother's Magazine* and *The Boys' World* on trains, in hotel rooms, and backstage, but mostly during her summer breaks from touring. This year, however, she and McRaye performed right up to the wedding. Now she must plunge into the neglected work to complete her 1910 commitments to the two magazines. She has promised eight boys' stories plus a four-part article on Mohawk silvercraft, which will be based on the symbols and legends behind the silver brooches that decorate her Indian costume.

She walks every day, rain or shine, usually to Stanley Park, where she stops for a brief rest at Siwash Rock, then marches triumphantly home again. Often she comes back with her skirts sodden with rain and seaspray, but she is still exhilarated by the venture. "It's the only way to chase the glooms away," she tells a young friend. "Go out, no matter what the weather!"

She is surrounded by friends, new and old, who come visiting at tea-time. Rosalind Webling Edwards comes frequently, sometimes with her three children, sometimes alone. The women belonging to the clubs that sponsored Pauline's recitals in the past come, too. One of them, Mrs. Frederick Cope, had "entertained" Pauline in her home in 1904, and now she takes it upon herself to mother her. Bertha Jean Thompson, a young elocution teacher from Brantford, who met Pauline years earlier on a camping holiday, arrives on her doorstep, homesick for family and friends. Without McRaye to fuss over, Pauline is looking for a new protégé and she opens her arms to this unhappy girl. Pauline is also introduced to the influential Isabel McLean, who writes a column for the *Province* newspaper under the pseudonym "Alexandra," and is persuaded to join the Canadian Women's Press Club, where she makes new friends.

When Chief Joe Capilano visits, he settles for an hour or so into one of the straight-backed chairs in Pauline's sitting room, often departing again without saying more than a half-dozen words. Pauline never prods him to speak, but sits wordlessly in his company. After several of these silent visits he suddenly says, "You would like to know this?" and launches into a Capilano legend, "a wondrous tale, full of strange wild poetry – the kind of folklore which soon will be heard no longer." For Pauline's benefit, he speaks in a mixture of Chinook and English, telling the stories that underlie both the history and the customs of his people. Sometimes, if there are other visitors present, he can be persuaded to tell again the story of his visit to London, laughing when he recalls Chief Basil's face as he caught sight of himself in the mirrored ceiling of the royal reception room. There is an urgency to his storytelling and to Pauline's listening. He is nearing sixty years of age at this time and is dying of tuberculosis.

Eileen Maguire leaves McRaye's tour in October and comes home to Vancouver. One of her first visits is to Pauline, who has been awaiting her return with a mixture of pleasure and dread. There is something about the singer's personality – "a whole-souled, Irish quality" – that allows Pauline to talk about things that she can't share with others, and there is something important now on which she needs advice. There is a lump in Pauline's right breast, a lump that has been growing slowly for as much as two years, but is now enlarging rapidly. She has not been to a doctor, partly because she still recalls her mother's instructions about allowing men to touch her, and partly because she has seen too many doctors during her bouts of rheumatic fever and erysipelas, but mainly because it was difficult to locate a doctor while she was touring.

Perhaps subconsciously she knows what the lump is, but since ladies don't discuss their anatomies, she has only bits of gossip to rely on. As soon as Eileen Maguire sees her, she knows something is wrong: Pauline has lost her matronly figure and her complexion has become pallid. But when Eileen learns about the breast lump, she is horrified and rushes her off to a doctor.

Thomas Ransom Biggar Nelles is only twenty-six, but he is the most qualified doctor in the city to undertake Pauline's care. A graduate of McGill University's medical school, he served at the Montreal General, then went to study at the New York Skin and Cancer Hospital. In Vancouver he is listed as a dermatologist, but in reality his practice is almost entirely cancer cases. Pauline's immediate trust in him, however, stems from another source: he comes from Brantford and is the son of old friends of her parents.

At this time the only treatment for breast cancer is a radical mastectomy operation. Unfortunately, this is only a delaying tactic since surgical procedures are not refined enough to allow removal of the entire cancer. And although radium has been used experimentally on cancers since 1900, radium treatments have not yet been attempted on humans. But neither procedure would be any help for Pauline. Dr. Nelles tells her that the lump is definitely cancer and it is advanced far beyond the operable stage. All he can do now is help her deal with the pain. Remembering the media circus when she was ill with rheumatic fever in Halifax and the daily press announcements on her condition, she swears Dr. Nelles and Eileen Maguire to secrecy. As long as she can prevent the world knowing about her illness, she will be able to keep her privacy and dignity. Like the heroes in the legends told by her grandfather, she makes up her mind to face death unflinchingly.

She writes now at a furious pace to earn her living and finance the days ahead when she can no longer work. Recognizing the special quality of the stories that Chief Joe has been telling her, she begins putting them into written form. She knows that the best market for them would be in some West Coast journal, but none exists. Two of the local newspapers, however, have magazine sections, and to test their acceptance, she takes the manuscript of "The Legend of the Two Sisters," which she had sold to *Mother's Magazine* earlier that year, to the office of Walter C. Nicol, owner of the Vancouver *Province* newspaper. Nichol pounces on the idea of being the first newspaper to run a whole series written by the famous Pauline Johnson, and he calls his magazine editor, Lionel Makovski, into his office.

"This is Princess *Tekahionwake* whom you probably know as Pauline Johnson of Canada's theatrical trails," Nicol says, introducing her to Makovski.

Makovski smiles incredulously. "Not 'A Pagan in St. Paul's'?" he asks.

Her face lights up. "The same," she says. "That was the best piece of prose I ever wrote! How do you know it?"

Then he explains that he had heard it quoted the evening after it was published in the *Daily Express*. He had been listening to a critic goad a young writer when the young man had turned on his tormentor and, to prove a point he was trying to make, had read out Pauline's article in full. Makovski never forgot it.

At this point, Nichol breaks into the conversation to explain that Pauline has a story that seems suitable for the *Province*, after which he excuses himself and leaves the office. For a few minutes more, Pauline and Makovski talk about London, then abruptly Pauline returns to business.

"I'm taking up your time, but I'll leave this story with you. If you can use it, I can follow up with others."

Makovski frowns at the title on the first page, and she hears the question he hasn't asked. "They are the mountain peaks on the North Shore that white people call the Lions, but the Indians call them the Two Sisters. I have written their story as Chief Joe Capilano told it to me." She turns to leave. "I am living on Howe Street. The number is on the manuscript. I am very pleased to have met you." And she walks out.

The magazine editor can't believe his luck. Only three years earlier he came from England after working on newspapers in Liverpool and London. Now thirty-five years old, he has been employed by Nichol for only a few months, but suddenly he has his hands on the most promising series any editor could hope for. He decides to give the stories first-class treatment with photographs to illustrate them. He chooses George Edwards to do the job.

Chief Joe Capilano dies in his sleep on March 10, 1910. On the 17th, the little church on the North Shore reserve is the scene of his burial service and the installation of the new chief, his son Mathias. Later, Chief Joe's coffin is carried from the church to the graveside in a procession led by the Indian Mission band. Here the final service is read and hymns are sung as whites and natives stand side by side to pay their last respects. When the coffin is lowered into the ground, it carries Pauline's spray of white lilies, the flower chosen by the Mohawk people to signify peace and power.

As she and Makovski stand by the grave, Pauline's eyes are dry. Then Makovski hears her speaking, and leaning closer, he hears her say, "I'm coming. I'm coming. I hear dem angels calling…poor old Joe." Then realizing that Makovski has overheard, she adds, "Well, it's the one thing we're all certain of, isn't it?"

Although Makovski has not been told of the cancer, he suspects something is terribly wrong because Pauline looks so unwell and often cancels appointments with him without explanation. Then, during the summer of 1910, the cancer spreads to her right arm and the spasms of pain are so intense that there are days, then weeks, when she cannot write. She falls behind in her writing commitments, and at last she has to tell Makovski that she cannot complete the series of legends she has promised him.

Makovski knows that she cannot afford to give up the income from the legends, and he comes up with a solution: he will transcribe the legends as she dictates them. As a result, throughout August and September he spends his evenings writing at the round Mission oak table while Pauline lies on the couch dictating. In this way the legends continue to appear regularly in the paper. In mid-October his help suddenly becomes unnecessary when Pauline begins a period of remission and is able to write once more herself. She completes more stories for boys and several for *Mother's Magazine* and finishes the last of the Capilano legends, "The Grey Archway," just before Christmas.

This period of remission is made even happier for Pauline because of Lucy McRaye's return to Vancouver to await the birth of her first child. For Pauline, this baby will be a surrogate grandchild, but Lucy's baby boy is born with a defective heart and lives only six weeks. McRaye, on tour in the Kootenays, never sees his son. When he receives word of the child's death, he writes a brief note to his wife, urging her to rejoin the tour as soon as possible. He encloses a five-dollar bill and tells her to go out and buy herself a new hat.

By this time, in spite of her efforts to retain her privacy, news of Pauline's illness has gradually spread. Whenever possible she has still been doing her own shopping and walking regularly in the west end, sometimes even as far as Stanley Park when her strength permits. But friends who come calling frequently find her incapacitated with pain or the morphine Dr. Nelles has prescribed for it. They share their concern with other friends.

Young Chief Mathias visits Pauline as his father did before him, and in the spring of 1911 she helps him organize a trip to Ottawa to bring his people's problems to the attention of the federal government. To give prestige to Chief Mathias's delegation, she writes a letter to Prime Minister Sir Wilfrid Laurier, asking him to receive the young man. Laurier writes back agreeing to meet with him and listen respectfully. Unfortunately, Laurier is defeated later in the year and his promises come to nothing.

During the early months of 1911 Pauline continues to give recitals from time to time with Eileen Maguire sharing the platform, but now, rather than putting the necessary energy into reciting one of her Indian poems, she reads, mostly from the legends. Or she sits to give informal talks about the legends and traditions of the Mohawks. Though almost always in pain, she remains cheerfully optimistic in front of an audience. But in June, a few days before a scheduled performance in the Fraser Valley community of Hammond, the pain is so intense that she has to beg off. The two young women who have organized the event substitute local talent instead and bring Pauline the profits of the evening, changed into gold pieces and tucked into a box of strawberries, the first of the season. Pauline, who is now almost penniless, is so touched by the gesture that she is unable to speak to thank them. This is the last time that she attempts to give a performance.

There is now no income from writing, either, as that has become impossible. And Chiefswood has fallen into such a state of disrepair that the last tenants have moved out, cutting off her share of that revenue. The only assets she has left are family heirlooms, and she prepares to sell these to pay the rent. She knows that in Vancouver, where everyone is upwardly mobile, there will be plenty of buyers. Friends tactfully intervene, paying the rent for her and buying food, but Pauline is proudly independent and will not accept this kind of charity for long.

A plan is hatched, however, to provide her with a steady income from her past writing endeavours. It is spearheaded by Alexandra, who assembles a committee at the home of the mayor, Charles Manley Douglas. Among those attending are members of the Canadian Women's Press Club, the Women's Canadian Club, Lionel Makovski and Bernard McEvoy of the *Province*, and Sir Charles Hibbert Tupper. They decide that they will publish the Capilano legends in book form and pay the profits into a trust fund for Pauline's continuing care. The Women's Canadian Club, led by Elizabeth (Mrs. Jonathan) Rogers, rents the Pender Auditorium for an evening of readings of Pauline's poems; the funds raised are enough to print the first thousand copies of the book. Over Pauline's vehement objections, the committee decides to call the book *The Legends of Vancouver* rather than *The Legends of the Capilanos* because they feel it will sell better with the name of the city on it.

In the meantime, Pauline is existing on the charity of friends. Hearing of her plight, an old friend in Brantford, Mrs. A. Hardy, canvasses that city's prominent people, and in the space of a few hours collects five hundred dollars. This gift arrives just before Christmas, by which time the first thousand copies of *Legends* – though poorly edited and only bound in paper covers – has sold out. Since Pauline's immediate needs are being met by the Brantford gift, the committee ploughs the book receipts back into the project, ordering another thousand copies – in cloth covers this time. Walter McRaye, returning to Vancouver for Christmas, volunteers to sell them as he tours. He persuades Pauline to autograph them, and whenever the pain in her arm allows, she inscribes book after book. Each of them sells for two dollars, a huge sum for a volume of Canadian prose in 1912.

In February 1912 Pauline's condition suddenly worsens, and Dr. Nelles recommends round-the-clock nursing care. Alexandra's committee scouts nursing homes and discovers a newly opened private hospital at the corner of Bute and Robson streets, not far from Pauline's apartment. Formerly the home of a fashionable doctor, it is run by Mrs. G.W. Moran. Pauline is given a sunny private room on the second floor, and her friends decorate it with her personal possessions.

But Pauline is not ready to die yet, and as spring comes, she gains strength. By June she is able to write her old friend Frank Yeigh. After thanking him profusely for his cheque covering donations from friends in Toronto, she writes:

> I am in hospital, but just now I am very well. I go out walking daily, and can take many little enjoyments when I am not suffering pain. My splendid young doctor is in the East for a much needed rest, and I promised him to remain in hospital until his return, although I have not had a heart "spasm" for seven weeks, and my arm is in good working order as you can see by my writing....

> I have just come through two months of being in bed, much of the time in extreme pain, but I am able to walk down town and in Stanley Park and by English Bay, able to shop and sew and write, and laugh and enjoy life for a little while before another of the inevitable spells catch me, and for all this I thank my good doctor and all my good friends who have put their hands deep into their pockets in Brantford and in Vancouver that I may have comforts and pleasures when I am too ill to wield a pen to earn my own "Muck-a-Muck" as the Chinook tongue hath it.... In my public life I must have builded better than I knew, my good old Yeigh-man, that my old townsmen should so regard and remember me.

That summer while the remission lasts, Pauline begins preparing her poems for publication as a collected edition. It will include all of the poems in *The White Wampum* and *Canadian Born*, plus a careful selection of those she has written since then, many of them never before published in journals or even recited in public. Two of them – "In Grey Days" and "And He Said Fight On" – reflect her thoughts on her illness and approaching death. There is much work to be done on all the poems, revising and correcting them, but she sets to work happily, and the committee prepares to add it to their publishing project. This time they agree with the title she has chosen: *Flint and Feather*. They are already busy gathering her boys' stories for a collection to be called *The Shagginappi* and a second volume to be called *The Moccasin Maker*, which will contain all of the stories submitted to *Mother's Magazine*.

The period of remission ends in mid-August 1912 and Dr. Nelles increases her morphine dosage once again. Whenever possible, she still walks in the West End, and even on a few occasions as far as Stanley Park, but she is barely recognizable now. She is, however, at peace, for her writing is providing her with independence once more, allowing her to depart from life with dignity and grace.

All her plans for her funeral and burial have been made. Having heard Pauline express a desire to be buried in Stanley Park, Clare Fitzgibbons of the Press Club has started the ball rolling by telephoning Elizabeth Rogers of the Canadian Club because Rogers' husband is the senior member of the Parks Commission. Stanley Park, however, is only leased by the city from the admiralty, and permission for the burial must be granted by Ottawa. No one has been buried within the park since white men began settling here, and the admiralty is anxious not to set precedents, but they finally suggest that permission might be possible on one condition: Pauline's body must be cremated.

When Mrs. Rogers comes to the hospital with this news, Pauline laughs. "Some people tell me I've got to be burnt anyway whether they bury me in a cemetery lot or not. Well, they can burn my body in this world to make certain of it! As for my spirit, that will be between the Great Tyee and myself."

Elizabeth Rogers sends word back to Ottawa and they are awaiting final permission when, on September

20, 1912, Pauline receives a visit from Arthur, Duke of Connaught, now Governor General of Canada. The nurses help Pauline dress in a new blue and gold kimono, and they drag out the old red cloak she wore with her Indian costume and drape it over the chair he is to sit on. Mrs. Moran ushers him and his aide-de-camp upstairs to Pauline's room for a half hour's visit. Before he leaves, Pauline asks if he will allow her to dedicate *Flint and Feather* to him, and the Duke agrees.

Outside he inquires if there is anything else he can do, and Lionel Makovski asks him if he can speed Ottawa's permission for the burial in the park as Pauline's time is growing short. "I'll see what I can do directly I return to Ottawa," the duke replies. Official approval is given a few weeks later.

In late fall Walter McRaye takes it upon himself to invite Eva Johnson to her sister's bedside. The two women have not set eyes on each other since Allen's wedding in 1907, and the letters between them since that time have been few, but McRaye is convinced that a reconciliation is not only possible but would be beneficial to Pauline. In response to his letter, Eva gives up her job in New York and travels west. At first it seems that he is correct; Eva and Pauline greet one another with warmth and affection and tears. But within days Eva begins demanding that Pauline sign her share of Chiefswood over to her immediately. Pauline assures her that it is already willed to her, but for Eva this is not enough; she wants it done before Pauline dies. Pauline stubbornly resists. Eva continues to nag.

Then Eva announces that she is going to take Pauline home to Brantford to end her days. Pauline will have none of this. She summons Makovski to her room and in front of the hospital staff makes him swear that he will not under any circumstances allow her – or her body after her death – to be taken east. Then reassured, she gives orders to Mrs. Moran to allow Eva to visit her only for limited periods at stated times.

Eva, forced out of the arrangements for her sister's death and burial, renews her sniping at McRaye, and out of range of Pauline's hearing, he snipes back. Eva harrasses Alexandra and her committee and antagonizes Elizabeth Rogers. But she does not leave town. Then just before Christmas, Pauline calls Eva to her bedside and graciously signs over her share of Chiefswood to her. She also gives her sister a mumber of family mementoes she has set her heart on as well as gifts Eva gave her long ago. Eva does not know what to make of this behaviour.

The first copies of *Flint and Feather* arrive from the printers in late December and Pauline struggles to autograph each one that is to go out for the Christmas trade, although every signature is paid for with excruciating pain. The seventh edition of *Legends of Vancouver* also arrives in time for Christmas sales, but she autographs only those that are destined for a personal order.

Throughout January and February 1913 Pauline clings to life with a terrible will, although she cannot use her right arm and her lungs are affected. Sometimes, heavily sedated, she spends the evening with friends or walks the streets near the hospital, but by the end of February, Nelles tells her friends that she cannot live more than a few more days. Death comes at mid-morning on Friday, March 7.

Vancouver Public Library

Following Pauline's funeral at Christ Church Cathedral in Vancouver, the cortege proceeds along Granville Street towards Mountain View Cemetery.

Epilogue

The Happy Hunting Grounds

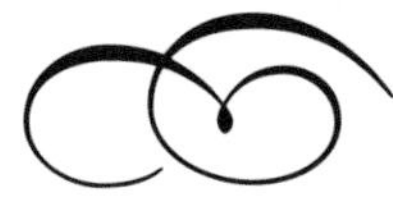

The afternoon sun streams through the great stained glass window of Christ Church Cathedral in Vancouver as the Reverend C.C. Owen reads the funeral service for Emily Pauline Johnson on Monday, March 10, 1913. In spite of Pauline's request that there should be no flowers at her funeral, flowers are banked high around her coffin. The church pews are packed with Pauline's friends and the elite of the city, and outside the streets are thronged with silent people. City offices have been closed for the afternoon to show respect for the dead poet, and all flags fly at half-mast.

As the service ends, the choir, singing "Crossing the Bar," leads the way for the pallbearers carrying the coffin outside to the waiting hearse. The dignitaries return to their carriages and the sombre procession sets out along Georgia Street between rows of stoically silent native people and weeping white men and women. Later that afternoon the coffin is deposited at Mountain View Cemetery for cremation.

On March 13 Elizabeth Rogers, who has organized the funeral according to Pauline's directions, is called to the funeral home to collect Pauline's ashes. Makovski accompanies her and together they are shown a tin can painted brown and tied with a white ribbon. The undertaker's clerk then attempts to open the can to show them the ashes, but the snugly fitting lid will not come off. He gets a letter opener and starts to pry at it.

Fearing it will suddenly fly off, Elizabeth Rogers cries out, "Don't do that! Don't do that! Leave it alone!" And she takes the can from him. "You'll spill Pauline Johnson all over the floor."

The can is placed between two silk cushions inside the small, crudely made concrete box that has been prepared by the city works crew. Makovski adds copies of *Flint and Feather* and *Legends of Vancouver*. The box is sealed and taken by automobile to Ferguson Point in Stanley Park. There a small crowd has gathered for the interment. Reverend Owen performs the burial service; then Walter McRaye reads Pauline's poem, "The Happy Hunting Grounds."

Into the rose gold westland, its yellow prairies roll,
World of the bison's freedom, home of the Indian's soul.
Roll out, O seas! In sunlight bathed,
Your plains wind-tossed, and grass enswathed.

Farther than vision ranges, farther than eagles fly,
Stretches the land of beauty, arches the perfect sky,
Hemmed through the purple mists afar
By peaks that gleam like star on star.

Laughing into the forest, dimples a mountain stream,
Pure as the airs above it, soft as a summer dream,
O! Lethean spring thou'rt only found
Within this ideal hunting ground.

Surely the great Hereafter cannot be more than this,
Surely we'll see that country after Time's farewell kiss.
Who would his lovely faith condole?
Who envies not the Red-skin's soul,

Sailing into the cloud land, sailing into the sun,
Into the crimson portals ajar when life is done?
O! Dear dead race, my spirit too
Would fain sail westward unto you.

B.C. Archives

The bronzed carving of Pauline's profile on her monument in Vancouver's Stanley Park faces her away from her beloved Siwash Rock.

Chronology of E. Pauline Johnson (1861-1913)

Compiled by Lynne Bowen

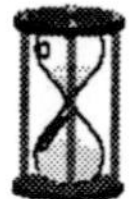

1712
The Tuscarora nation joins the Mohawk, Oneida, Cayuga, Onondaga, and Seneca Nations to become the Iroquois or Six Nations Confederacy, begun in legend by Hiawatha; a senate decides on matters of common interest.

1755
Irish immigrant Sir William Johnson is appointed superintendent of the Six Nations Iroquois.

c. 1758
At a mass baptism in Niagara, William Johnson gives his surname to a child named Jacob (Pauline's great-grandfather).

Johnson and Her Times | **Canada and the World**

1763 (Canada and the World)
Royal Proclamation reserves Indian "hunting grounds" and sets the basis for future treaties between the Crown and Aboriginal Peoples in British North America.

1775-1783 (Johnson and Her Times)
Chief Jacob (Tekahionwake) Johnson fights beside Joseph Brant, a Mohawk war chief and protégé of Sir William Johnson, against the American rebels.

1775-1783 (Canada and the World)
The Six Nations fight beside the British in the American Revolutionary War; when the Americans win independence, the Six Nations lose their lands, but the British grant them a 228,000-hectare reserve straddling the Grand River near Niagara in Upper Canada.

post 1784 (Johnson and Her Times)
Mohawk George Martin (another of Pauline's great-grandfathers) and his Dutch wife Catherine Rolleston Martin (adopted daughter of Chief Teyonnhehkewea) move to the Grand River settlement; their first child is Helen (Pauline's paternal grandmother).

1784 (Canada and the World)
Joseph Brant leads Mohawk loyalists to Grand River.

1791 (Canada and the World)
Under the pressure of thousands of Loyalists seeking refuge in British North America from the American Revolution, the Constitution Act creates the provinces of Lower and Upper Canada.

1792 (Johnson and Her Times)
John Johnson (Pauline's paternal grandfather) is born to Chief Jacob Johnson and his wife.

Johnson and Her Times	Canada and the World
1812-1814 John Johnson fights beside the British in the battles of Queenston Heights, Stoney Creek, and Lundy's Lane during the War of 1812.	**1812-1814** During the European war against Napoleon, the United States (U.S.) declares war on Britain and attacks Canada; the War of 1812 ends in a stalemate.
1816 John Johnson having married Helen Martin, their son, George Henry Martin Johnson, (Pauline's father) is born.	
1824 Emily Susanna Howells (Pauline's mother) is born to Reverend Henry Charles Howells and Mary Best Howells in Bristol, England.	**1824** Lord Byron, English poet, dies.
	1826 First lyceum provides public lectures and debates in Massachusetts.
	1829 The Six Nations cede land for the white village of Brantford on the Grand River.
1832 Mary Howells having died, Rev. Howells remarries and takes his family to Ohio.	**1832** Sir Walter Scott, Scottish poet, dies.
1837 George Johnson leaves school in Brantford to serve as a despatch rider during the rebellion in Upper Canada.	**1837** Rebellions in Lower and Upper Canada. Victoria becomes Queen of Great Britain and the Empire.

Johnson and Her Times

1842
The British force the Six Nations Senate to award a nonhereditary chieftancy to John Johnson; he is also given the new post of speaker of the Six Nations Senate and the title *Sakayengwaraton* (Smoke).

1845
Emily Howells goes to the Six Nations Reserve to live with her sister and brother-in-law; George Johnson also lives with the family and works as an interpreter.

George Johnson's mother selects him to be a Mohawk chief; he receives the name *Teyonnhehkewea*.

1853
Emily Howells marries George Johnson on August 27; according to Canadian Law, Emily and her future children are Indians.

1854
Henry Beverly Johnson (Pauline's brother) is born.

1856
Helen Charlotte Eliza (Eva) Johnson (Pauline's sister) is born.

Johnson family moves into Chiefswood near Brantford.

1858
Allen Wawanosh Johnson (Pauline's brother) is born.

Canada and the World

Johnson and Her Times	**Canada and the World**
	1860 Ernest Thompson Seton, author and naturalist, is born in England. Cariboo Gold Rush begins in British Columbia (B.C.)
1861 Emily Pauline Johnson born in Chiefswood on March 10; she is named Emily after her mother and Pauline after the Emperor Napoleon's only sister.	**1861** Beginning of American Civil War.
	1862 William Barker makes a huge gold strike and founds Barkerville, B.C.
1865 Because of his opposition to corrupt timber buyers, George Johnson is attacked and suffers permanent scarring to his face.	**1865** End of American Civil War. Pullman sleeping cars first appear on U.S. railroads.
	1867 Ontario, Quebec, Nova Scotia, and New Brunswick join to form the Dominion of Canada.
1868 George Johnson escorts Arthur, Duke of Connaught, into the Mohawk Church to be made a chief of the Six Nations; the red blanket he kneels on becomes a Johnson family keepsake. Johnson begins her formal education at home with a governess.	

Johnson and Her Times	**Canada and the World**
	1869 Louis Riel leads the Red River Rebellion; he imprisons Charles Mair, who escapes and returns to Ontario to agitate against the Métis and help found the nationalist movement, Canada First.
1870 Johnson goes to school on the Six Nations reserve.	**1870** Manitoba joins Canadian Confederation. Canadian towns and cities begin to build opera houses to give touring theatre and musical companies places to perform.
	1871 British Columbia joins Canadian Confederation. First of the "numbered treaties" is signed with Prairie Indian nations. Emily Carr, future painter and writer, is born in Victoria.
1872 Johnson studies at home with her mother; she reads the poets Scott, Browning, Longfellow, Tennyson, Byron, Keats, and Milton; her earlier ill-health having improved, she learns how to paddle her canoe, "Wildcat." Charles Robert Lumley Drayton (Johnson's future fiancé) is born in Barbados.	

Johnson and Her Times	Canada and the World
1873 George Johnson is attacked and left for dead.	**1873** Prince Edward Island joins Canadian Confederation. Canada establishes the North-West Mounted Police (NWMP). Donald Smith, Manitoba politician, joins the company that will build the Canadian Pacific Railway (CPR).
1874 Governor General Lord Dufferin and Lady Dufferin visit Chiefswood.	**1874** Women in Ontario found the Woman's Christian Temperance Union, which promotes women's suffrage, sex hygiene, Prohibition, and mothers' allowances. Summer concerts and lectures begin at Lake Chautauqua, New York, and become travelling shows.
1875 Johnson enrolls as a boarder in Brantford Collegiate; she proclaims her Indian-ness.	**1875** *Trial by Jury*, the first Gilbert and Sullivan comic operetta, opens in London, England.
1876 Walter Jackson McCrea (Johnson's future stage partner J. Walter McRaye) is born in Merrickville, Ontario.	**1876** The Toronto Women's Literary Club is founded as a screen for women's suffrage activities. American cavalrymen under Lt.-Col. George Custer are massacred by the Sioux and Cheyenne at the Little Bighorn River.

Johnson and Her Times

1877
Johnson finishes school and returns to Chiefswood to write poetry and visit friends and relatives while she waits to meet a suitable husband.

1878
George Johnson is attacked a third time and is left psychologically damaged.

1879
The Marquis of Lorne and his wife, the Princess Louise, visit Chiefswood.

Johnson writes her first full-length poem, "My Jeanie."

1883
Johnson's poem, "The Sea Queen," is printed in *The Week*; Charles G.D. Roberts (poet and animal-story writer) is impressed and begins a twenty-five-year-long correspondence with Johnson.

Canada and the World

1877
The surrender of Sioux chief Crazy Horse marks the end of the American Plains Indian wars; Sioux chief Sitting Bull escapes to Canada.

1882
Treasure Island by Robert Louis Stevenson is published.

1883
In Toronto, Goldwin Smith founds *The Week*, which provides writers with a prestige market.

U.S. frontiersman W.F. Cody (Buffalo Bill) organizes the "Wild West Show"; Sitting Bull has returned from Canada and is one of the attractions.

Johnson and Her Times	**Canada and the World**
1884	**1884**
Four of Johnson's poems are published in *Gems of Poetry*.	*Huckleberry Finn* by Mark Twain is published.
Chief George Johnson dies of erysipelas.	*Old Spookses' Pass, Malcolm's Katie, and Other Poems* by Ontario poet Isabella Valancy Crawford is published at her own expense.
1885	**1885**
Unable to maintain Chiefswood, Johnson, her sister, and her mother rent the house to a tenant and move into Brantford.	Métis and Indians, led by Louis Riel, rebel against the Canadian government in the District of Saskatchewan, Northwest Territories.
Johnson meets Mlle. Rhea, a Belgian actress known for her magnificent gowns; Rhea advises Johnson to join the Brantford Dramatic Society.	Donald Smith drives the last spike of the CPR at Craigellachie, B.C.
1886	**1886**
Johnson's grandfather, Chief John "Smoke" Johnson, dies; Pauline Johnson assumes her great-grandfather's Indian name: *Tekahionwake*.	The first through passenger train on the CPR arrives in Port Moody, B.C., on July 4; completion of the railway allows entertainers to travel more economically and quickly.
At the unveiling of a statue to Joseph Brant, Johnson's "Ode to Brant" is read by W.F. Cockshutt.	Charles Mair writes the play *Tecumseh*, which Johnson says "enriche[s] Canadian Indian literature."
	1887
	Queen Victoria's Golden Jubilee.

Johnson and Her Times	**Canada and the World**
1890 Johnson meets the Weblings (an English family of recitalists) in Brantford. Johnson sends her poems to John Greenleaf Whittier (American poet and abolitionist), who praises them.	
1891 Johnson begins to write and sell articles in quality literary magazines.	
1892 Novice impresario Frank Yeigh organizes Johnson's first public recital in the Art Gallery at the Academy of Music, Toronto, on January 16. In November, Johnson wears an Indian costume on stage for the first time and begins to perform with Owen Alexander Smily, an English pianist and impersonator. Johnson begins to write articles that explain Iroquois ways.	**1892** John Greenleaf Whittier dies.
1893 By summer, Johnson and Smily are a team.	**1893** *Low Tide on Grand Pré*, by Canadian poet Bliss Carman, is published. *The Magic House and Other Poems*, by Canadian poet Duncan Campbell Scott, is published. *The Canadian Magazine* is launched in Toronto.

JOHNSON AND HER TIMES

1894
Johnson has become the darling of the entertainment pages in Ontario, New Jersey, New York, and Massachusetts.

In April, Johnson sails to England to find a publisher.

Johnson meets titled and influential Londoners and attends several glittering social events. John Lane, a partner in the Bodley Head, the most prestigious poetry publisher in England, agrees to publish Johnson's book of poetry.

Johnson and Smily tour western Canada and travel by train to the West Coast.

Henry Beverly Johnson dies.

1895
Johnson and Smily complete another western tour.

In July, Johnson's *The White Wampum* is published in England, Canada, and the U.S.; Canadian reviews are good, but British reviews are mixed.

In the fall, Johnson and Smily tour the Maritimes.

CANADA AND THE WORLD

1894
The first of *The Jungle Books* by Rudyard Kipling is published.

Beautiful Joe by Margaret Marshall Saunders is published. It becomes the first Canadian book to sell more than a million copies.

1895
Peggy, Rosalind, and Lucy Webling begin a three-year tour of Canada.

Johnson and Her Times	Canada and the World
1896	**1896**
Johnson establishes her home in Winnipeg's Manitoba Hotel.	Clifford Sifton becomes federal minister of the interior and superintendent general of Indian affairs in the newly elected Liberal government of Wilfrid Laurier; Sifton's immigration policies open the Prairie provinces to large numbers of immigrants.
Having toured the entire country, Johnson and Smily embark on their first American tour; Johnson notes the audiences' lack of culture.	Donald Smith founds Royal Victoria College for Women at McGill and is appointed high commissioner for Canada in Britain.
Gold is discovered in the Klondike.	
1897	**1897**
Because she refuses to share top billing, Johnson's partnership with Smily breaks up; they never speak again.	Donald Smith becomes Lord Strathcona.
In Winnipeg, Charles Drayton meets and pays court to Johnson.	The British Empire celebrates Queen Victoria's Diamond Jubilee.
J. Walter McRaye arranges to meet Johnson and becomes her partner for a short tour.	Presence of NWMP makes the Klondike gold rush the most orderly in history.

JOHNSON AND HER TIMES

1898
On January 25, Johnson announces her engagement to Drayton.

Johnson meets Charles Mair, who sees in her a "pagan yearning."

Emily Johnson dies; Johnson closes her mother's house.

Johnson loses touring time and income because of illness; in the fall her new agent, Thomas E. Cornyn, sends her alone on a tour of fifty small Prairie settlements; she is depressed, and illness has depleted her savings.

1899
In a year marked by constant touring and lukewarm reviews, Johnson loses her belongings when the Manitoba Hotel burns down; just before Christmas, however, she gives a polished and confident performance in the Winnipeg Grand Opera House.

CANADA AND THE WORLD

1898
Wild Animals I Have Known by Ernest Thompson Seton is published.

1899
In a move that divides Canadians along French/English lines, Canada sends troops to South Africa to fight in the Boer War; Lord Strathcona funds Lord Strathcona's Horse.

Johnson and Her Times

1900
His family opposed to his marriage to Pauline Johnson, Drayton asks to be released from the engagement to marry someone else.

Johnson gives benefit concerts for Canadian regiments going to the Boer War.

Johnson's new manager, Charles Wurz, disappears with her money and cancels her Maritime tour when she becomes ill with rheumatic fever; after a month's recuperation, Johnson tours to pay her hotel and medical bills.

Canada and the World

1900
Most propertied women in Canada are now allowed to vote in municipal elections.

Doctors begin to use radium experimentally to treat cancer.

The Commonwealth of Australia is created.

Daily Express, London, is first published.

Johnson and Her Times	**Canada and the World**
1901	**1901**
Johnson is forced to borrow money from Frank Yeigh when she is stranded while touring Ontario.	Queen Victoria dies and is succeeded by her son, King Edward VII.
Johnson tours with Clara Cornyn, a concert pianist and the wife of Thomas Cornyn, who has become Johnson's manager again; Johnson and Clara perform before the Governor General of the British colony of Newfoundland, but succeeding recitals are poorly attended.	*The Impressions of Janey Canuck*, the first of four popular books by Emily Murphy under her pen name, Janey Canuck, is published.
Johnson asks Minister of the Interior Clifford Sifton to buy her the rail tickets to get to Montreal from the Maritimes.	
Johnson cancels Cornyn's contract and asks J. Walter McRaye to be her stage partner and manager.	
In December, Johnson becomes ill with erysipelas; she loses her hair and her face is disfigured.	
1902	**1902**
On June 30, Johnson and McRaye give a recital for Regina's elite that was originally intended to coincide with the coronation of the King.	Boer War ends.
	The coronation of Edward VII is postponed because the King requires an emergency appendectomy.
At Calgary, Alberta, Johnson and McRaye give a number of recitals to CPR passengers stranded by bridge washouts; the tour goes on to play to sold-out houses in the Kootenays.	King Edward VII crowned on August 9.
	Glengarry School Days by Ralph Connor (pen name for Charles W. Gordon) is published.

Johnson and Her Times	Canada and the World
1903 Johnson's second book of poems, *Canadian Born*, is published; critics are disappointed.	
During the summer, on a camping and canoeing trip in Ontario, Johnson begins to write adventure stories for boys.	
1904 Johnson meets Royal North-West Mounted Police (RNWMP) Inspector Charles Constantine and his wife, who provide material for her stories.	**1904** The word "Royal" is added to NWMP name to recognize the distinguished service of NWMP men in the Boer War.
During Johnson and McRaye's tour of B.C. they perform in Barkerville, and share the stage with B.C. Premier Richard McBride at Lac la Hache.	
1905 Johnson and McRaye tour Ontario, New York state, New Brunswick, Alberta, Saskatchewan, and Manitoba.	**1905** Alberta and Saskatchewan become provinces of Canada.
Johnson asks Ernest Thompson Seton to find a buyer for her wampum belt, a Six Nations relic.	

JOHNSON AND HER TIMES	**CANADA AND THE WORLD**
1906	
Johnson and McRaye sail for England aboard the CPR's *Lake Champlain*; they attend Lord Strathcona's garden party; "A Pagan in St. Paul's," the most famous of Johnson's articles on Mohawk life, is published in the *Daily Express*; Johnson meets with Chief Joe Capilano and two other chiefs who are in London to place their grievances before the King; Johnson makes lasting impression on English poet Algernon Swinburne.	
1907	**1907**
Johnson's tour of Jamaica is cancelled when an earthquake levels Kingston, Jamaica, in January.	Lyceums and chautauquas merge and tour North America providing evangelical religion, education, and entertainment.
Johnson goes to England for a six-week holiday.	W.H. Auden, English poet, born.
Slayton Lyceum Society hires Johnson and McRaye for a gruelling ten-week tour of the American plains states, where Indians are treated as lesser beings.	Rudyard Kipling wins the Nobel Prize for Literature.
1908	**1908**
Bob Edwards, publisher of the *Calgary Eye Opener*, stages a hoax to prove discrimination against Johnson as a woman poet.	*Anne of Green Gables* by L.M. Montgomery is published.
Johnson takes the CPR to Vancouver, where she visits Chief Joe Capilano; she paddles her canoe along the harbour and renames Lost Lagoon in Stanley Park.	

Johnson and Her Times

1909

On August 23, in Kamloops, Johnson and McRaye make last public appearance together; he marries actress and dancer, Lucy Webling, 26, and they leave on the first McRaye Company tour.

Johnson settles in Vancouver; she is diagnosed with untreatable breast cancer; she begins to put Capilano's stories into written form but eventually has to dictate them to Lionel Makovski (magazine editor of the Vancouver *Province*) because of pain in her arm.

1910

Chief Joe Capilano dies.

Johnson joins the Canadian Womens' Press Club.

Canada and the World

1909

Algernon Swinburne dies.

1910

National Council of Women speaks out for Canadian women's suffrage.

King , dies and is succeeded by his son, King George V.

Mark Twain and Leo Tolstoy die.

Johnson and Her Times	**Canada and the World**
1911	**1911**
Johnson gives recitals with contralto Eileen Maguire.	Prime Minister Laurier's government is defeated in the federal election.
Johnson helps Capilano's son, Chief Mathias, organize a trip to Ottawa and arranges visit with Prime Minister Laurier.	Arthur, Duke of Connaught, becomes Governor General of Canada.
When pain makes it impossible to support herself, Johnson's friends organize a committee to publish *The Legends of Vancouver*.	
1912	**1912**
Living in a private hospital, Johnson prepares *Flint and Feather*, a collected edition of her poems; *The Shagginappi*, her boys' stories; and *The Moccasin Maker*, her *Mother's Magazine stories*.	SS *Titanic* sinks.
The Duke of Connaught visits Johnson in hospital; Charles Mair also visits.	
Harassed by her sister Eva, Johnson signs over her share of Chiefswood.	
1913	**1913**
Johnson dies on March 7; on March 10, the day of her funeral at Christ Church Cathedral, all city offices are closed for an hour and flags are flown at half-mast; her ashes are interred in Stanley Park.	Poet Duncan Campbell Scott becomes deputy superintendent of Indian Affairs.
	Suffragette demonstrations in London.
	1914
	World War I begins.

Johnson and Her Times	**Canada and the World**
1915 Using seed money from Johnson's royalties, the Vancouver *World* launches a subscription fund to buy a gun for the Canadian army.	**1915** Canadian troops in Europe are short of guns.
McRaye and Lucy separate.	
	1918 World War I ends.
	All female citizens (except status Indians) aged twenty-one and over eligible to vote in federal elections.
1922 Large stone with a bronze medallion is installed to mark Johnson's grave.	

Sources Consulted

CHARLESWORTH, Hector, *Candid Chronicles*, Vol. 1. Toronto: Macmillan Co. of Canada, 1925.

FOSTER, Mrs. W. Garland, *The Mohawk Princess: Being Some Account of the Life of Teka-hion-wake (E. Pauline Johnson)*, Vancouver: Lions' Gate Publishing Company, 1931.

HOWAY, Frederic W. and SCHOLEFIELD, Ethelbert O.S. *British Columbia from the Earliest Times to the Present*, Vancouver: S.J. Clark and Son, 1914.

JOHNSON, Emily Pauline, "Among the Blackfoots," *Toronto Globe*, 2 August 1902.

———, "The Cariboo Trail," *Toronto Saturday Night*, 13 October 1906.

———, "Coaching on the Cariboo Trail," *Canadian Magazine*, 42, February 1914.

———, *Flint and Feather, the Complete Poems of E. Pauline Johnson (Tekahionwake)*, Toronto: Hodder and Stoughton, 1969.

———, "From the Child's Viewpoint," Chapter 1. *Mother's Magazine*, May 1910. Pp. 30-31.

———, "From the Child's Viewpoint," Chapter 2. *Mother's Magazine*, June 1910. Pp. 60-62.

———, "Iroquois of the Grand River," *Harper's Weekly*, 23 June 1894.

———, Legends of Vancouver. 8th ed. Vancouver: Saturday Sunset Press, 1913/

———, *The Moccasin Maker*, With an Introduction by Sir Gilbert Parker and an Appreciation by Charles Mair. Toronto: William Briggs, 1913.

———, "A Strong Opinion on the Indian Girl in Modern Fiction," *Toronto Sunday Globe*, 22 May 1892.

JOHNSON, Emily Pauline, and SMILY, Owen, "There and Back," *The* (Toronto) *Globe*, 15 December 1894.

KEEN, Dorothy and MCKEON, Martha as told to Mollie Gillen, "The Story of Pauline Johnson, Canada's Passionate Poet," *Chatelaine*, February and March 1966.

KELLER, Betty C. *Pauline, A Biography of Pauline Johnson*, Vancouver/Toronto: Douglas & McIntyre, 1981.

MACKAY, Isabel Eccleston, "Pauline Johnson: A Reminiscence," *Canadian Magazine*, July 1913.

MCRAYE, J. Walter, *Town Hall To-Night*, Toronto: Ryerson Press, n.d.

MAIR, Charles, "An Appreciation," *Canadian Magazine*, July 1913.

MAY, J. Lewis, *John Lane and the Nineties*, London: John Lane, the Bodley Head, 1936.

OTTAWA, Public Archives of Canada, MG 27, II D 15, Clifford Sifton Papers: letters from Johnson dated 1900-1901.

———, Public Archives of Canada, MG 30, D 58, Frank Yeigh Papers: letters and clippings concerning Johnson, two poems by Johnson, and one letter from Johnson.

———, Public Archives of Canada, MG 22, A 14, Gertrude O'Hara Papers: a letter from Johnson to Frank Yeigh.

SHEARMAN, T.S.H, "Pauline Johnson's Shy Sister Devoted Life to Her," Vancouver *Province*, 25 November 1939.

STEVENSON, Jean, "The Real, Lovable, Tender, Fun-Loving Pauline Johnson," Vancouver *Province*, 6 March 1932.

WEBLING, Peggy, *Peggy: The Story of One Score Years and Ten*, London: Hutchinson and Co., 1924.

Index

Aberdeen, Earl of (Arthur Hamilton-Gordon), 34
Alexander, Sir George (actor/manager), 103, 122
American Slayton Lyceum Society, 103, 109
American Canoe Association, 26
American Revolutionary War
See War of Independence
"And He Said Fight On," 134
Argyll, Duke of (John Douglas Sutherland Campbell), 97
See also Marquis of Lorne
"As Red Men Die," 5, 37
"At the Ball," 79
"Avenger, The," 17, 36, 50

Banff, Alberta, 47, 83
Barkerville, B.C., 147, 88
Bernhardt, Sarah (French actress), 38
Betourmay, Albert, 57
Bijou Comedy Company, 63
Blake, Lady Helen, 97, 103
Bodley Head, The, London (publisher), 36, 38, 153
Boer War, 69, 155-158
Boissevain, Man., 44
Bonaparte, Chief Basil, 100
Boston *Herald*, 115
Boys' World, The, magazine, 123
brain fever, 80
Brandon, Man., 45
Brant, Joseph, 5, 144, 151
Brantford, Ont., 7-10, 22, 26, 30-31, 40, 42, 44-46, 61-63, 89, 104, 108, 124, 126, 132, 134-136, 145-146, 149, 151-152
Brantford *Courier*, 60
breast cancer, 126-127, 128-130, 133-137
Brockville, Ontario, 108
Brophy's Point, Thousand Islands, Ont., 26
Bryan, William Jennings, 114

Calgary, Alberta, 47, 67, 69, 83-84
Calgary *Eye Opener*, 87, 159
Calgary *Daily News*, 87
Camp McKinney, B.C., 84
Campbellton, N.B., 75
Canada Permanent Loan company, 57
Canadian Pacific Steamships, 93, 102
"Canadian Born," 70, 85
Canadian Born, 85, 134, 158
Canadian Magazine, 89, 152, 163-164
Canadian Pacific Railway (CPR), 149
Canadian Women's Press Club, 125, 132
Cannington Manor, Sask., 49
Capilano legends, 125, 127-130, 132
Capilano, Chief Mathias, 116, 129-130
Capilano, Chief Joe, 90, 100-102, 116-117, 125, 128-129, 159-160
Cariboo country, B.C., 87-89
Carman, Man., 44
Cataraqui Canoe Club, 26
"Cattle Thief, The," 112-113
chautauqua, 103, 108-116, 149
Chiefswood (Johnson family home), 7, 9, 33, 66, 70, 85, 91,

97, 123, 131, 136-137, 146-147, 149, 150-151, 161
Chinook language, 101, 125, 134
Christ Church Cathedral, Vancouver, B.C., 122, 138-139, 161
Clarendon Hotel, Winnipeg, Man., 58
Cleveland, Ohio, 113, 121
"Coaching on the Cariboo Trail," 89, 163
Coal Creek, B.C., 84
Coal Harbour in Burrard Inlet, Vancouver, B.C., 117
Colorado, 114
Columbia, Penn., 45
Connaught, Arthur, Duke of, 21, 33, 136, 147, 161
Constantine, Mrs., 86, 158
Constantine, Inspector Charles, 86, 158
Cope, Mrs. Frederick, 124
Copp, Clark Company, Toronto (publisher), 38
Cornyn, Thomas E. (Pauline's third manager), 63, 74-75, 155, 157
Cornyn, Clara, 74-75, 157
Cranbrook, B.C., 68
"Cry from an Indian Wife, A," 2, 37, 112

Daily Express, The (London, England, newspaper), 98-100, 103, 128, 156, 159
Dakotas, the, 58, 69
Dartmouth, N.S., 71
Davidson, John (editor of *The White Wampum*), 36, 38
Didsbury, home of the Beckton brothers at Cannington Manor, 49
Dominion Illustrated, The, 18, 25
Donegal, Marchioness of, 97
Douglas, Mayor Charles Manley of Vancouver, 132
Drayton, Lydia née Howland, 81
Drayton, Philip, 59-62
Drayton, Charles Robert Lumley (Pauline's fiance), 54, 57-63, 69, 81, 148, 154, 155, 156
Drayton, Mrs. Philip, 62
Drummond, William Henry (author of *The Habitant*), 58
Du Domaine, Ernest, 57
Duse, Eleanora (actress), 38

Edmonton, Alberta, 67, 86, 116
Edward VII, King of England, 82, 90, 94, 157, 160
Edwards, Bob, 87, 159
Edwards, Rosalind née Webling, 104, 124, 153
Edwards, George, 104, 122, 128
Empress Hotel, Victoria, B.C., 47
Erysipelas, 7, 80, 151

Fairview, B.C., 85
Fenwick, Maggie Bar, 14
Fernie, B.C., 84
Filpaynem, Chief Charlie, 100
Fitzgibbons, Clare, 135
Flint and Feather, 134, 136-137, 140, 161, 163
Forget, Mme. Henrietta, 81-82
Forget, Lieutenant-governor of Northwest Territories, 81-82
Fort Macleod, Alberta, 46
Fort Saskatchewan, Alberta, 86
Fraser, Malcolm, editor of the *Daily Express*, 98-99

Gleichen, Alberta, 82
Globe, The, 2, 13, 18, 42, 48, 61, 82
Golden, B.C., 47

Graham House, Havelock, Ont., 73-74
Grand River, Ont., 7, 16, 144, 145
Grand River Reserve, Ont., 33, 144
  See also Six Nations Reserve
Grand Trunk Railway, 32
Greenwood, B.C., 84
"Grey Archway, The," 130
Guardian, The (newspaper), 48-49

Halifax *Herald*, 71
Halifax, N.S., 71-72, 107, 127
Hamilton, Ont., 7, 9, 62, 80, 108, 122
Hammond, B.C., 131
Handscombe, Charles, 56-58
"Happy Hunting Grounds, The," 140-141
Hardy, Mrs. A., 132
Harper's Magazine, 86
Harrisburg, Penn., 32
"Haunting Thaw, The," 86
Havelock, Ont., 73
Haymarket Theatre, London, England, 103
Hiawatha, legendary founder of the Six Nations Confederacy, 34, 143
Hotel Vancouver, Vancouver, B.C., 47, 116-117

Illinois, 49, 115
"In Grey Days," 134
"In the Shadows," 17
"Indian Medicine Men and their Magic," 18
Indian Associations, 62, 111, 115
Indian Wars, 111, 150
Indiana, 49, 111, 114
Iowa, 49, 114

Johnson, Henry Beverly (brother), 7, 45, 146, 153
Johnson, Helen Charlotte Eliza "Eva" (sister), 7, 11, 20-21, 31-32, 62, 66, 70-71, 73, 78, 93-94, 136-137, 146, 161
Johnson, Emily Pauline
  burial, 135-137, 139-140
  and canoeing, 12, 16, 26-27, 31, 43, 44, 78, 86, 116-117, 148, 159
  costumes, 14-15, 20-21, 22, 26, 33, 38, 40, 42, 49, 96, 112, 123
  death, 137, 161
  and elocution techniques, 14, 24, 67-68, 131
  engagement to Charles Drayton, 54, 59-60, 62-64, 69, 155, 156
  and final tour, 121-122
  and finances, 9-10, 29-30, 38, 42, 50-51, 70-74, 75, 85, 87, 88, 91-93, 107, 123-124, 129, 131, 132-133
  first public appearance, 1-5
  heritage, 2, 5, 6, 16, 19-20, 34, 60, 112
  and humour, 22, 24, 50, 68-69, 84
  and illness, 11, 16, 25-26, 38, 59, 62-63, 72, 79-80, 125-137, 160
  as the Mohawk Princess, 20, 32, 109
  and performances, 1-5, 16-19, 24-27, 33, 34, 50, 56-57, 64, 67-69, 70, 79, 84-85, 112-113
  physical appearance, 2-3
  and racial intolerance, 19-20, 60, 111-113
  retirement, 108-109, 117-118, 123
  and reviews, 48-49, 86, 97
  as *Tekahionwake*, 15, 32, 48, 127
  and touring trials, 49-53, 72-73
Johnson, Chief George Henry Martin (father), 2, 6, 144
  as chief, 20

and erysipelas, 7, 80, 151
as government agent, 19
Johnson, Floretta Katherine née Maracle, 108
Johnson, Chief John "Smoke" (*Sakayengwaraton*) (grandfather), 5, 21, 34, 92, 111, 146, 151
Johnson, Allen Wawanosh (brother), 7, 15, 31-32, 61, 70-71, 78, 108-109, 123, 136, 146
Johnson, Emily Susannah née Howells (mother), 6-7, 10-11, 31, 42, 61, 145, 146, 155
Johnstown, N.Y., 93

Kamloops, B.C., 87, 122, 160
Kansas, 114
Kawartha Lakes district, Ont., 86
Keith Rowse Entertainment Agency, 94
Kelly's Hotel, Barkerville, B.C., 88
Kerby House, Brantford, Ont., 31, 108
Kingston, Jamaica, 107, 159
Knebworth Hall, Hertfordshire, 95-96
Kootenays, the, B.C., 68, 84-85, 87, 116, 130, 157

Lac la Hache, B.C., 76, 88, 158
Lamson Wolffe and Company, Boston (publisher), 38
Lane, John (publisher, the Bodley Head), 36-37, 153
le Gallienne, Richard (writer), 36
"Legend of the Two Sisters, The," 127
Legends of Vancouver, The, 132, 137, 140, 161
Leighton, Sir Frederic (artist), 37
Leland Hotel, Winnipeg, 81
Lethbridge, Alberta, 46
Liverpool, England, 32, 38, 128
"Lodge of the Law-Makers, The," 99
London, Ont., 80
London, England, 9-10, 28-38, 41-43, 49, 55, 82, 90-95, 97-104, 107-109, 116-117, 122, 125, 128, 149, 153, 156, 159, 161
Lorne, Marquis of, 30, 97, 150
See also Argyll, Duke of
Lost Lagoon (*see* Coal Harbour)
lyceum, 103, 109-110, 114-115, 145, 159

M.A.P., literary journal, 95
Maguire, Eileen, 117-118, 122, 125-127, 131
Makovski, Lionel, magazine editor of the Vancouver *Province*, 127-130, 132, 136-137, 140, 160
Manitoba Free Press, 56
Manitoba Hotel, Winnipeg, Man., 56, 59, 62, 64, 154-155
Manitoba Morning Free Press, 63
Manitou, Man., 44
Massachusetts Indian Association, 115
Massey Hall, Toronto, 70
Maugham, Somerset, 103
McAdam Junction, N.B., 72
McBride, Premier Richard of B.C., 76, 88, 158
McCrea, Walter Jackson, 57, 149
McEvoy, Bernard, editor of the Vancouver *Province*, 132
McGillicuddy, Daniel, 87
McGillicuddy, Owen E., 87
McLean, Isabel "Alexandra", 124
McRaye, Lucy née Webling, 103-104, 121-122, 153, 160, 162
McRaye, J. Walter, 57-58, 66, 74-75, 76, 77-89, 91-94, 96-97, 101-104, 107, 110-111, 113-116, 120-

122, 124, 130, 133, 136-137, 140, 149, 154, 157-160, 162
See also McCrea, Walter Jackson
Medicine Hat, 45, 82
Michigan, 49
Minnesota, 69
Missouri, 114-115
Moccasin Maker, The, 135, 161, 164
Mohawk language, 16
Mohawk people, 5, 6, 8, 16, 20, 111, 129
Mohawk Princess, the, 20, 32, 109, 163
Mohawk warriors, 5, 16-18
Montreal, Quebec, 75, 107, 157
Montrose, Duchess of, 97
Moosomin, Sask., 49
Moran, Mrs. G.W. (Private hospital administrator), 133, 136, 137
Morang Publishing Company, Toronto, 85
Morden, Man., 44
"Mother o' the Men," 86
Mother's Magazine, 108, 123, 127, 130, 135, 161, 163
"Mrs. Stewart's Five O'Clock Tea," 68-69
Muskoka Lakes Canoe Association, 27

Nanaimo, B.C., 47
Nebraska, 114
Nelles, Dr. Thomas Ransom Biggar, 126-127, 130, 133, 135, 137
Nelson, B.C., 84
New York, 32, 58, 59, 62, 85, 89, 93, 109, 111, 126, 136
New, E.H., 48
Nicol, Walter C., publisher of the Vancouver *Province*, 127
North-West Mounted Police (NWMP), 46, 149
See also Royal North-West Mounted Police (RNWMP)

O'Brien, Harry, 27, 44, 45, 50, 73, 78, 86
Ohio, 49, 145
Okanagan Valley, B.C., 85, 87, 116, 122
Orillia, Ont., 41-42, 79-80
Ottawa *Citizen*, 79
Ottawa, Ont., 9, 25, 62, 68, 70, 75, 79, 130, 135-136, 161
Outing Magazine, 86
Owen, Reverend C.C., 139

"Pagan in St. Paul's, A," 99-100, 102, 127-128, 159
Parker, Sir Gilbert, 95, 98, 108-109, 164
Pearson, Sir Arthur (newspaper publisher), 98, 103, 108
Peterborough, Ont., 73-74, 91
Phoenix, B.C., 84
Pincher Creek, Alberta, 46
Pittsburg, Penn., 121
Port Arthur, Ont., 43
Prince Albert, Sask., 116

Qu'Appelle, Sask., 69

Rainy River, Ont., 89
Rat Portage (Kenora), Ont., 43
"Red Girl's Reasoning, A," 25-26, 79
Regina, Sask., 61, 81-82, 157
Retallack, B.C., 84
rheumatic fever, 63, 72, 126-127, 156
"Riders of the Plains," 70
Ripon, Lord, 34
Roberts, Charles G.D., 14, 98, 150

Rod and Gun Magazine, 87
Rogers, Elizabeth (Mrs. Jonathan), 132, 135, 137, 140
Rossin Hotel, Toronto, Ont., 42
Rossland, B.C., 84
Royal Hotel, Nanaimo, B.C., 47
Royal North-West Mounted Police (RNWMP), 86, 108, 158
See also North-West Mounted Police (NWMP)

SS *Lake Erie*, 108
SS *St. Paul*, 109
SS *Lake Champlain*, 93, 159
SS *Etruria*, 32
SS *Lake Manitoba*, 102
San Francisco, Calif., 41, 85
Sandon, B.C., 84
Saskatoon, Sask., 116
Sault Ste. Marie, Ont., 43
Scott, Clement (critic), 35-36
Seton, Ernest Thompson, 23, 92, 116, 147, 155, 158
Shagginappi, The, 135, 161
Sheridan, General Philip, 111
Shipman, Ernest (Pauline's second manager), 42-43, 51, 63
Sifton, Clifford, 70, 75, 154, 157, 164
"Silent News-Carrier, The," 99
Siwash Rock, Stanley Park, 124, 142
Six Nations Confederacy, 34, 143
Six Nations Reserve, 7, 19, 146, 148
See also Grand River Reserve
Six Nations Senate, 5, 19, 146
Smily, Owen Alexander, 23-26, 30, 31, 42-53, 55-56, 152, 154
"Song My Paddle Sings, The," 12, 16-18, 27, 49
Souris, Man., 44
Southampton, England, 93, 109
St. Joseph, Missouri, 114-115
St. Stephen, N.B., 72
St. Paul's Cathedral, 99
St. John's, Newfoundland, 75
St. Patrick's Hall, St. John's, Newfoundland, 75
Stanley Park, Vancouver, B.C., 123-124, 130, 134-135, 140, 142, 159, 161
Steinway Hall, London, England, 94-95, 97
Strathcona, Lord (Donald A. Smith), 95-96, 100-101, 155, 159
Sudbury, Ont., 42-43, 62, 81
Swinburne, Algernon, 97-98, 159-160

Terry, Ellen (British actress), 38, 122
"There and Back," 48, 164
Thompson, Bertha Jean, 124
Toronto, Ont., 1, 7, 10, 13, 21, 24, 27, 38, 42-43, 59, 62-63, 85, 86, 109, 133, 150, 152
Toronto Saturday Night, 14, 18, 88, 163
"Trail to Lillooet, The," 103
"Train Dogs," 86-87
Trout Lake, B.C., 84
Tupper, Sir Charles Hibbert, 132
Tupper, Sir Charles, 34, 37, 97

Vancouver, B.C., 47, 67-68, 90, 104, 116-118, 122, 125-140, 142, 159, 160
Vancouver *Daily World*, 47
Vancouver *Province*, 67, 127-128, 132, 160, 165
Vernon, B.C., 85
Victoria, B.C., 47, 100, 122, 148
Wabash Railroad, 114
Waller, Lewis, 122

wampum belt, 21, 48, 92-93, 158
War of 1812, The, 5, 145
War of Independence, The, 5, 111, 144
Warrington, Fred, 14
Washington, Kate (Pauline's cousin), 62, 80, 108
Watson, William (actor/manager), 37
Watts-Dunton, Theodore, 97
Webling, Peggy, 104, 165
Week, The, 2, 150
West Selkirk, Man., 44
White Wampum, The, 48, 97, 134, 153
White, Percy (writer/editor), 36
Wilde, Oscar (writer), 37
Winnipeg, Man., 44-45, 54, 56-58, 61, 62-64, 69, 81, 116, ,154
Women's Canadian Club, 132, 135
Woodstock, N.B., 72-73
Worford, Countess of, 97
Wurz, Charles, 71-72, 156

Yeigh, Frank (first manager), 2, 4, 5, 8-11, 13-17, 19-24, 31, 42, 43, 73-74, 133-134, 152, 157
Yeigh, Kate née Westlake, 5
Young Men's Liberal Club of Ontario, 1

Printed in October 1999
at Marc Veilleux printing,
Boucherville (Québec).